Looking Back

Looking Back

Mania Salinger

FERNE PRESS

Salinger, Mania.
Summary: Memoir of a Polish Jewish woman's life before the
Holocaust and her survival in Nazi work camps and concentra-
tion camps.

ISBN: 1-933916-60-5
I. Salinger, Mania. II. Looking Back.
I. Holocaust. II. Memoir. III. Poland. IV. Bergen Belsen.
V. Auschwitz. VI. World War II.
Library of Congress Control Number: 2006933768

FERNE PRESS

salingermgmt@hotmail.com

Table of Contents

Dedication

With love and gratitude to my daughters Susan, Joanie, and Debbie, and to my son-in-law Jon, for their love and support, for always being there with patience and encouragement when I need them.

To my late husband, Martin, who, with wisdom, understanding, support, and love, led me to a new life.

Acknowledgment

I would like to extend my thanks to my editors, Sarah and Marian, for their enthusiasm and dedication.

To Selma Silverman, administrator of the Holocaust Center, who nudged me to publish my memoirs.

To Gail Cohen, Tour Coordinator of the Holocaust Center, for assigning me the "best" groups for my Survivor presentations.

To Rabbi Rosenzveig, founder of the Holocaust Center, whose vision and dedication brought the Center to life.

To Sir Martin Gilbert, for his encouragement and for sharing with me his fantastic records and facts of the Holocaust.

Prologue

I had many doubts about writing my memoirs. Remembering and revisiting the past is not an easy task. It would not have been possible without the motivation and encouragement of my children. It was Debbie who urged me to start, more than twenty-five years ago now. She supported me with much confidence. And it was Susie who urged me to resume again, when I initially left off, years later. Joani always offered help in all directions.

Despite my doubts and anxieties and poor literary skills, I could not deny that I had an unquenchable desire to share my story. Hitler succeeded in obliterating a whole and very rich kind of life. It will never be again.

I want very much to pass on to my family a fraction of that old life, a sense of it . . . memories of it. I want them to know what life was like for my family. For *our* family. I wanted to leave more than just a family tree with empty names.

Even after I overcame my initial doubts and had resolved to write my story, I had to face many questions and dilemmas. Should I reveal my innermost thoughts? Should I awaken what I thought was safely buried deep in my mind—painful memories from so very long ago?

What do I remember? Where should I start? I certainly didn't want my book to be only a gruesome account of the times of war. I knew that that was not, and is not, what I care to dwell upon. But I knew also that I would have to relate details about those times because, of course, they are so important in my life story.

How, I wondered, would I be able to describe the years of brutality, sickness, and starvation that I had to endure? I was lucky. In the midst of all of it there were at times miracles. I did encounter some Germans who were not brutal Nazis, but were instead fearful collaborators, following orders, anxious about their own safety.

To one such German I owe my life.

I wrote this book in stages. In 1979 I had surgery on my foot and my bed-ridden status gave me opportunity, at last, to start writing down some of the memories of Poland and also our life during occupation. It wasn't until years later that I was ready to revisit my memories through the war years. I shelved the book again for many years and only reached for it again recently when thoughts of publishing entered my mind.

I read it with such mixed emotions. There was so much that I wanted to add, so much more that I remembered. And so, I shall continue with my journey, and hope to leave a family legacy for my children, grandchildren, and the generations that will come.

The Beginning

I was born February 23, 1924, in the city of Radom, in Poland. I was not born in a hospital, but was delivered at home by a midwife. When I emerged, I was still encased in my caul, the fetal membrane, which had not broken during birth. In later years my mother told me that, according to superstition, being born with the caul intact is a prediction of good luck. I believed her, and always assumed that I would be blessed with good fortune. My mother saved that caul for many years, until we were forced to move to the Ghetto and had to leave our belongings behind. Now, decades later, when I look back on all the blessings and good luck that I have had in my life, I wonder if it was all the hand of destiny, since I was born in a caul.

I was the second baby girl born to my parents. I presume that this must have been a source of anxiety, and even disappointment, to them because it meant that they would have to start planning for another dowry. Dowries were very important in Poland, and parents had to start saving for them very early in their daughters' lives. Despite this fact though, what I remember of

My family in Poland. I am about 10 years old.

my parents' treatment of me was their great love, generosity, and affection.

My mother was a beautiful and sensitive person. She was charming and vivacious, and I always felt a great closeness with her. I have many memories of her. My papa was a gentle, quiet man, and a bit more remote in my memory than my mother. He never punished us, I never even remember him raising his voice.

My sister, Rella, is three years older than me. She was a pretty girl with a light complexion and quiet and mature mannerisms. She tells me that she was not happy with the arrival of a baby sister. Other than my sister, I had one other sibling. My little brother, Jacob, was born when I was six years old. He was a bright, beautiful boy with big black eyes. We called him Kubek. He was the baby of the family and the only boy. He loved to draw, was loving and affectionate, and was pampered by everyone. Both my parents and my darling little brother did not survive the war. My sister survived—the only one from my immediate family.

All of us kids grew up in a generally loving atmosphere. I don't remember ever being spanked or punished, and yet we gave my parents our full respect and love. We got early training in values and sensitivity to other human beings. Jewishness—as in the Jewish ethic—was never taught to us directly by our parents; we learned it form watching their example. It became our way of life. We were told that we should always strive to be a *mensch*: a true human being—a good, decent person. That is what every person should be. I have not forgotten the lessons of my parents, and I live by them still. I instilled into my children the value of being a *mensch*, and I hope those Jewish ethics will be an important part of all my future generations.

I don't come from one of the famous eastern European *shtetl* (small towns) that are featured in so many books, poems, and movies. Radom was, by European standards, a large city. Before the war, it had a population of about one hundred twenty thousand. Radom was an industrial city, a hub, mainly known for the leather industry.

My father's family lived mainly in Radom. My mother's family lived mainly in Warsaw and the nearby surrounding area. Radom is about fifty miles south of Warsaw. I have only vague memories of all my aunts and uncles. I do remember some faces but not many names. Both of my parents came from large families. Nearly all of them perished in the war.

I don't know why so little is written about the life of Jews in larger cities. Radom was a vibrant city with an active Jewish community of about thirty-five thousand people. Most of the Jewish people lived in one area of the city, but Jews of better means mingled with Christians and lived in mixed neighborhoods in more desirable locations. These were the neighborhoods with better school systems. We lived in one such area. Our building was located in the center of Radom, on Zeromskiego 48. The area was considered very good—a privileged area for a large city. When I returned to Poland in 1979, thirty-eight years since the last time I'd been on Zeromskiego, I was happy to see the area had been made into a beautiful boulevard, closed to automobiles, with mounds of flowers for the pedestrian traffic to enjoy.

Our apartment building was located in a mixed but mostly non-Jewish area. It housed about fifteen or twenty families, and five or six of them were Jewish. Most city-dwellers lived in apartment buildings. One-family homes were located on the outskirts of the city and the people that lived there were usually those that

My home in Poland: Radom, Zeromskiego 48.

owned or worked in outlying factory and didn't want to worry about a long commute.

Much has been written about the unfriendly relationship between the Polish Christians and Jews. Poland was known to be the most anti-Semitic country in the world. (Before the war, there were thirty-five thousand Jews living in Radom. Now, there are none, and anti-Semitism is as prevalent as it was before.) In most areas of society there was a total separation between Christians and Jews. In our building, however, residents prevailed in friendship and congeniality. All the children played together in the backyard and in one another's homes. Never, however, did Christian kids socialize with us beyond the confines of our apartment building.

The area we lived in was prestigious. The state offices were located a block away, and there was a very fashionable restaurant across the street. The name of this restaurant was Wiezbicky, and it was known throughout Europe. The restaurant had a sign on the door: "No dogs or Jews allowed." Once during my frequent talks at the Holocaust Center, I was asked by one of the students to give him an example of anti-Semitism in Poland. I told him about that sign. It was enough. During my return visit to Radom many years later I could not resist the urge to go into the restaurant which, under the same name, is now a candy store. I was an American by then.

We sometimes saw (a rare sight!) a movie star traveling by car and stopping in this restaurant. Only movie stars and high government officials could afford cars. We used to run across the street and touch the car with great admiration and awe. Not even in my wildest dreams, and surely I was a dreamer, did I imagine I would ever own one. I remember once a car drove up to the restaurant with music coming from a radio in it. I was amazed. From then on I had a secret wish to someday own such a car, and live in a suburb near a lake. How amazed I would have been to know that, indeed, both of those wishes would be fulfilled. Life is full of wonderful surprises!

We were also very lucky because our building not only had a great backyard (such space was a precious rarity) but also had a large and beautiful orchard adjoining the building's property. It was fenced off but it belonged to the owner of the apartment building, Mr. Mazurkiewicz, who was a nice man. I am surprised that I actually remember his name. He must really have been a very nice man. I remember that Mr. Mazurkiewicz allowed us to play in the orchard and to pick fruit. The orchard was quite large—it even had a gazebo in it. Beyond the orchard was a spacious and beautiful state park stretched for an area of about two square miles. We kids from the building made an opening in the fence that separated the orchard from the park, so we had our own little shortcut.

When I think back now, it's funny which incidents from my childhood stand out in my memory. My first memory dates back to when I was about four years old. Some kids from our apartment building formed a club. My older sister, Rella, was in this club but they would not let me join because I did not know how to read. I must have been a determined child. Right then and there, at that moment, I decided to teach myself to read. And I did. I accomplished my goal by the age of five. Then, I was very eager to start school. My mother, with a great deal of persistence and pushing through red tape and various tests, got me accepted to elementary school—first grade—one year early. There was no kindergarten class in Poland, nor were there nursery schools.

Throughout my school years, I did very well.

By school age, I was called Marysia by my friends. Later in life it became Maniusia (an affectionate, diminutive form of Mania). I was never known as Mania at school, play, or home. I dislike the name Mania. To this day I am sorry that I did not change it when I arrived in the United States. My husband and I just could not think of any name to change it to. Every one I suggested, he disliked. So we left it Mania. I am still called Maniusia by my childhood friends.

I always felt a great closeness with my mother. I resembled her so much in looks and temperament. (When my daughter Debbie was a little girl she saw a picture of my mother and she said, "That's my mom when she was a grandma.") Her influence fills my childhood. We had a special kind of relationship, one that is hard for me to describe. It was not friendship—for I kept my personal secrets to myself. Yet it was a lot more than just the usual mother-daughter love. There was a special affinity, as if we recognized in each other a kindred spirit. In character and attitude, I am so very much like my mother! She was energetic and vivacious and very social. I have been told that, as a young woman, she won some beauty pageants. She was very talented too. She sang beautifully (I still remember the Jewish lullabies), sewed, embroidered tablecloths, knitted sweaters, and made holiday decorations. When I was sent home with lengthy school projects that required sewing and hemming and the like, she would always finish them for me! Her name was Szaindla. My daughter Susan is named after her.

Sometimes now, when I reflect back on the relationship that I had with my mother, I see that she favored me, and I assume it was because I was so like her. Perhaps she experienced the things that I did—the fun and the friends and the education and the adventures—through me, as if she were living them herself. I contemplate the mother-daughter relationship often, and wonder about my own daughters. Is every daughter a bit of—a part of—her mother? Does every mother live through her lifetime of memories as she watches her daughter grow up and mature? I have always tried to give a lot of myself to my daughters, but nonetheless I am often plagued with anxious regrets and feelings of insecurity.

Our papa was a wonderful father. He owned a shoe factory in town. I visited the factory often and was always fussed over. When we became old enough to care, we

A hug for my sister Rella.

children had the privilege of choosing any custom-made shoe design we wanted. I usually insisted that Papa not put my shoe design into production, because I wanted to own the one and only original shoe of that type, in the whole city! The factory had a peculiar leather smell, and it would cling to my father even when he was at home. My father built for my sister Rella and me an outstanding dollhouse. I remember it so vividly! It took him months to create, and it was absolutely magnificent. It had five rooms all filled with miniature hand-made furniture (mostly made out of leather—from the shoe factory of course!) with carpets, wallpaper, bathroom, and all.

My sister Rella (Relcia, we called her at home) resembles my father in every way. Rella and I are contrasts in looks and temperament. When we were young, we mostly ignored each other. What a turnaround our relationship took in our adult life. During and after the war we became close, and to this day we have a loving and supportive relationship.

Although we had a live-in maid, housework still took a lot of time and effort. We only had one little electric burner, which we did not use very much because electricity was very expensive. Most of our cooking was done on a wood stove. Of course there were no large refrigerators—we had a small ice box—and all water we used for laundry or bathing had to be heated on the stove. Mother was always busy, yet she managed to spend a lot of time with us while we were growing up.

When we were small we had a nanny who at times had a hard time keeping up with our mischief.

The winters are very cold in Poland—a lot of dry, freezing weather. Homes were heated by tile ovens built into the walls so that they could heat two rooms at once. Charcoal was fed into the ovens continuously during the day, but at night the fire would die out. It was always very cold when we got up in the mornings, and often we had to wash in a basin of cold water since it took a long time to heat the water on top of the wood stove.

Mother was up very early every morning, with us. She would fix our breakfast—including the hot cocoa which was a must every morning, and our vitamins (cod liver oil, which I hated, but had to take since I was so skinny . . . believe it or not!) Mom made sure we were ready for school and checked our schoolbooks and packed our lunches. There were no hot lunches at school then.

Milk was delivered daily to our apartment. I remember the old, tired lady who schlepped those large

cans of milk (just as you see in "Fiddler on the Roof").
My mother always invited her in for a cup of tea. Milk,
then, was boiled before we drank it. In the summer,
ice was also delivered daily for our little ice box. Food
storage was difficult in the hot weather, but in the cold
winter we could keep food on the balcony or in a locker
in the basement of the building.

I never helped with the housework, since we had
help, but I did participate in some household duties
that seemed fun to me. I often shopped with my mother
at the open farmer's market. In my mind's eye I can
see her again, so vividly, tasting the butter of several
farmers. But she almost always bought it from the same
German farmer. Presumably, he had the very best.

Women shopped for groceries daily since there
wasn't much cold storage. There was an art to buying
poultry. Mother used to blow between the feathers of the
chicken or goose in question to see how yellow its skin
was, which foretold how fat the animal was. The fatter,
of course, the better. We always bought live birds and
after the purchase Mom headed to the kosher butcher to
have it killed. Then the bird had to be plucked, cleaned,
slated, koshered, and, finally, cooked. We had a kosher
home. Nearly all the Jews in Poland did.

My mother taught me many shopping and housekeeping tips in preparation for the future. Of course,
in the modern world of technology and pre-packaged
food, I have never had a chance to use any of her skills.

I have strong memories of washday. Once a month
we had two days of complete turmoil. Besides my mother
and the maid, a special laundress was also hired for this

event. The linens and all the laundry were scrubbed by hand on scrub boards in huge basins, and then they were rinsed and boiled on top of the stove. The steam would fill the whole apartment and I still remember the choking dampness and the smell—I hated both. By the time I was in high school I had a solution to avoid washday at home. I would move in to my girlfriend Hanka's house for those two days, and we made sure with our mothers that our washdays did not coincide.

The laundry was then hung to dry in the attic of our apartment building. The attic was very clean, and had dozens of specially prepared laundry lines. This attic was accessible to anyone. We often played there as kids because it was a fun area. But, it was also easily accessible to thieves. I remember how upset my parents were one time when Mother found her whole laundry stolen.

The living room furniture was always covered with white sheets, so I can't recall any of the furnishings in our home except for my parents' twin brass beds (everyone slept in brass beds). I do remember that there was a sofa (rather more like a daybed) in the dining room which could be used as an extra sleeping facility. In the house there were two bedrooms and a tiny room in the back of the kitchen where the maid slept. Besides the dining room, the kitchen also had a small eating area.

By housing standards of the area, our apartment was an adequate-sized living space for the five of us (plus the maid) but during long and cold winters, when one spent so much time indoors, I remember that there really wasn't any room for privacy, especially since friends and family were always dropping by.

Spring in Poland is sunny and warm and, when you are young, the sunny days seem to last forever. A girl-friend of mine, who lived in the same building, had an apartment balcony that faced the backyard. We spent many happy hours there when the weather was nice. We both loved playing with dolls—even when we were older and supposed to be too old to play with dolls anymore. We would sometimes cover the outside of the balcony with a blanket so no one could see us from the outside and tease us! I remember when this apartment with the balcony became available for rent later on. I was just dying for us to move there, but my parents were afraid to take on the additional financial burden of higher rent.

One spring our apartment manager offered a prize to the child who would plant and grow the prettiest flowers in our backyard. What a project that was! Every kid was allotted an area of about six by eight feet to work with. At the time, I was probably about six or seven years old. I well remember carefully designing my area into a heart which I then planted with rows of different flower seeds. I watered my garden plot daily, watched it grow, and talked lovingly to my growing flowers. I was so proud of it! That summer our building must have had the prettiest backyard garden in the whole city.

Life was simple. We did not have many luxuries. I wanted so much to learn to play the piano. Two of my friends did, but we didn't own one. Oh how spoiled we all are now! We take all of our choices and opportunities so much for granted.

Holidays, however, were always very special and very festive. Sabbath was always special too. I remember the cleanliness of the home, the smell of specially pre-pared food (even the poorest families cooked a special meal on the Sabbath), and, most important to us children, the Shabbat surprise that Dad would bring. We usually waited for his arrival from work on Friday afternoon and mobbed him, searching his pockets for toys and sweets. My mother would plead that we not eat the sweets until after supper.

Saturdays were very special. Dad attended services at the synagogue every Saturday morning, as most Jews in Poland did. When he returned, we would be waiting, dressed in our Sabbath best and ready for our weekly walk through the neighborhood. I remember those walks so clearly—they were something I looked forward to each week, these wonderful Sabbath promenades. Our whole family would stroll down Zeromskiego's main street, greeting friends and exchanging invitations for visits later, for tea.

Dad went to the synagogue on Shabbat only, but prayed daily. Dad said prayers every morning. I have come to the conclusion that our forefathers were brilliant because, as doctors are discovering now, prayer is not only good for the soul, but also for your health. Deep concentration relaxes the heart and reduces high blood pressure, so I am told.

Our synagogue had no Sunday school, no Hebrew school, and no youth services. The kids were more or less ignored (very orthodox kids attended the yeshiva). But we grew up with a lot of "Jewishness" despite the fact that we were surrounded with Christianity. The

Jewish traditions of our home and the celebrations that we shared with neighbors and friends always reminded us of our faith.

At home we spoke only Polish because my parents were afraid that otherwise we children would acquire an accent. My parents spoke Yiddish when they didn't want us to understand. My sister picked up a lot of that language, but I didn't learn it until I was in the United States and learned it from friends and family.

Our classes in school always started with a Catholic prayer. Poles are all Catholic. They had a priest teaching religion in school. During those classes, we, the Jewish kids, had to walk out into the hall. But once a week, during the Catholic children's religion hour, we had a teacher who would come in to instruct us in Jewish religion and Jewish history. As I remember, he had a hard time controlling us. We were always goofing off. One time in particular I remember . . . I had just learned the British national anthem from my neighbor, and I taught it to my Jewish schoolmates. We would walk into our Jewish-learning class singing "God Save the King," just to irritate our poor teacher. We sang it with great vigor even though, of course, not one of us understood a word of English.

Our parents hired a private tutor to come to our house and teach my sister and me Hebrew and some Yiddish. He was a dirty old man. I hated him so much that nothing he taught us penetrated into my mind. My sister Rella remembers a lot more. She learned to follow prayers and write some Hebrew. I draw a blank. I am not sure why.

I am told that I was pretty as a girl, which I can sub-
stantiate only with a joyful memory I have from when
I was about six or seven years old. One of our neighbors asked Mother if she could enter me in a children's
beauty contest. Reluctantly, Mother gave her permission. I don't remember the details of the event, but I
won it. Far more important to me, evidently, than the
event itself was a moment that happened afterward,
because this I remember clearly. We returned late in the
evening, far later than I was usually out. The neighbor
rang the bell at the entrance gate our building, and the
doorman opened the door (every apartment building's
entrance was locked up in the evening). Before entering,
I slipped back on the winning crown and the queen's
cape which I had received after the judging. I will never
forget the expression on my mother's face, looking
down at us from the open window. She watched us walk
up the path. Her eyes filled with tears. At the time, I
felt terrible for causing my mother to cry, even though
I didn't know what I had done. It took me a while to
figure out that tears of happiness and pride look the
same as tears of sorrow.

When I returned to Poland in the '70s, I found the
photographer who had taken pictures of us, the winners
of the contest. I wanted very much to find the pictures,
but it would have taken days to sort through his basement collection. My Polish friends dissuaded me from
doing this. It was too dangerous, they said, for a Jew to
be alone with a Pole for such a long period of time in
this anti-Semitic country.

Oh but we kids were a mischievous bunch! I remember a prank we did at one of the last festivals of Sukkot, in Radom. This festival lasts for seven days and it commemorates the dwelling in which the Jews lived in the wilderness after leaving Egypt. The Jewish tenants of our building built a Sukkah in the backyard. This Sukkah is a shed without a roof and its purpose is to unite people in prayer. The Sukkah is roofless so that we can look up at heaven. The Sukkah is covered with fruits and with greens, to celebrate the harvest. All the Jewish families ate their evening meals out at the Sukkah during the week of the celebration. It was festive and traditional. One evening, after everyone had finished their dinner, one older man stayed on alone. He wanted to pray, undisturbed.

Before everyone had left, a friend and I climbed up into a tree nearby. It was very dark and quiet on that late fall night. I looked down from my perch at the old man, praying devotedly, and in a whispery, faraway sounding voice—as I imagined God might sound—I called his name. Low, but loud enough for him to hear clearly. He got so excited, this poor man. He prayed more fervently, bowing deeply, uttering his prayers more loudly. At first we were overwhelmed with pride at our success. Then we realized that we had gotten ourselves in a trap! We would have to stay up in the tree until the old man finished—for if he caught us climbing down, we'd surely be punished severely. The old man, his devotion fueled by our prank, prayed for a very, very long time. And we stayed up in that tree, getting cold and stiff, for just as long. Perhaps for the rest of his life he truly believed that he had heard God speak to him. And for the rest of my life I shall have a guilty conscience!

Our parents were relatively well off financially, but they lived in anxiety about the dowries that they would have to provide for their daughters. This was a worry that could plague a family for a lifetime, and it inspired my parents to skimp and save. I always laughed and told my parents that my husband would marry me for love, not for money. If only they could have lived to see the time when I kept that promise!

My mother's mother, our grandmother, lived in a small town near Warsaw and visited us from time to time. She was a very slim, darling woman, but the hard life had left her looking tired and much older than her age. My mother's father had died in his early life, at the age of about thirty-five. He had been a rabbi in a smaller city near Radom. He had been respected and loved, I was told, and he traveled all over the country giving counsel and attending conferences. He had gotten pneumonia on one of those trips and died soon after. I never knew him. After that my grandmother had, without any money, managed to raise her large family of five children. It had been very difficult. All the kids worked from an early age, and somehow got educated. There was no Social Security or welfare in those days.

Most of my aunts and uncles on my mother's side lived in or near Warsaw. One brother emigrated to South America; one brother moved to Paris. Everyone on that side of the large family, except the family in South

America and Genia and Leon (cousins who escaped to Russia), perished during the war (Cousin Leon married my sister after the war). Despite the distance separating them, my mother was especially close with her brother from Paris. When the war broke out she made us memorize his address, "just in case we are separated," she said. After I married Marty and before coming to the US I went to Paris to try to find my uncle and his family, but none had survived.

Our father, whose given name was Tobias (called Tovy by his family) was born a twin. He was the first-born and his twin brother died in infancy. Papa had had many siblings—I think the total was six sisters and two brothers. Several lived in Radom, two lived in Warsaw. We saw them frequently. Only two sisters survived the war—an aunt who eventually settled in Israel (she escaped through Russia) and one who came to the United States and lived in Pittsburgh. This one miraculously escaped from the Warsaw ghetto and survived the camps, although she lost her children and her husband.

We visited the families in Radom often and they visited us, and at times we traveled to Warsaw to see family there. Although we saw one another frequently, it was always in small groups, not the enormous family gatherings that are traditional in the United States. Generally each family dined alone, as was the case with most other families in Eastern Europe. Perhaps this was because no one could accommodate large crowds in their apartments, but I also think that it was because food was a very expensive commodity in Poland. It might easily have constituted one half or more of a family's total budget. Even my grandparents seldom had dinner with us. At times we served cold cuts to guests, but usually guest food was tea, cake, and cookies.

We were very close with my grandparents on my dad's side. They lived fairly close. My grandmother I only tolerated. I remember her as being always grouchy, and a bit frightening. But my grandfather, Eli, I adored. He was a rare human being, a jewel. I used to stop at their home almost daily after school for a few minutes to see him. I would sit on his lap and listen to stories and jokes—he had a seemingly endless supply. Sometimes I had only enough time to give him a quick hug and kiss. He was always cheerful and had an exceptional sense of humor. He never answered a question with a straight answer. He would always respond with something like, "Well, I'll tell you a little story . . ." He had a cure for every sickness and a solution for every problem, all of which he minimized with his gentle joking. We all adored Grandpa Eli. I did especially. And I think that of all his grandchildren living in Radom, I was his favorite. I am so lucky that my grandson Eli Martin is named Eli after him, and Martin after his grandpa Martin. Little Eli Martin inherited the best genes from both. What a wonderful combination in this loving and delightful little boy.

About a year after Hitler invaded Poland, Grandpa Eli visited us one day in the ghetto (thankfully he and my grandmother had already lived in the area which became the ghetto, so they had not needed to move from their home) and said cheerfully, "Well, I don't feel like struggling through this horrible war. I don't feel well today, besides. I have lived a long and happy life, and I have a strange feeling that I'll go to heaven tonight." He looked well and healthy, and was certainly strong enough to walk to and from our house. He asked my father if he would like to send along a letter to his grandfather up above because, he said, "I think I'll see him tonight." Always joking, that was my grandpa. No matter how grim the circumstances, they did not stifle his humor. That night, he died peacefully in his sleep. He did not take his life.

***

I remember those times, the years of my childhood, with nostalgia that is almost like envy. It was a good life, and a simple life of the kind which will never return. When I remember those years with keen longing, and everything I recall seems so rosy, I wonder if it is possible that, through the filter of memory and nostalgia, I am remembering only the happy times and blocking out the sad ones?

We lived with anti-Semitism daily. We simply accepted it and did not imagine that life could be different. We were Jews, and knew we would always be treated as inferiors by the Christians. It was a fact. Also, we knew that we were in peril. We took it for granted that during Christmas and Easter we kids were not allowed to go outside alone. Too dangerous, we could have been beaten.

For most of my childhood, however, I did not experience much anti-Semitism directly. My family lived in harmony, and even in friendship, with our Christian

Visit to Poland with the Kubicka family.

neighbors. We were especially close with the Kubickas, a Christian family who, later on in the war, proved to be friends of the truest kind. Mrs. Kubicka was the greatest cook. She never failed to invite us to taste all her specialties. Her pastries were mouth-watering. On Christmas there were always gifts for us under their tree. As later events would prove, the Kubickas were among the small minority of thoughtful and liberal Polish people. I remember my mother saying that Mrs. Kubicka was born in Russia, and that was why she was not the "normal" anti-Semitic Pole.

In the spring of 1936 I took exams for the purpose of entering high school. That was when I encountered my first decisive incident of anti-Semitism, in my city of Radom. Radom had only one state-supported school, which one could attend at a nominal cost. A student had to qualify to attend—pass the tests and get selected from among the many other students hoping for acceptance. The other high schools were privately owned and expensive (in this day and age tuition would amount to about six or eight hundred dollars a month). There was also one private Hebrew high school, which was even more expensive. Only a small percentage of kids in Poland could afford a high school education beyond the state-supported school, and that group formed the "elite" of the youth.

I passed the required exams with flying colors. I qualified for admission to the state-supported high school. Of the two hundred freshmen who got accepted annually, only two Jews were accepted. The Jewish population in our city was approximately thirty-five thousand, out of a total population of one hundred twenty thousand. You can see that the numbers do not match up—the number of Jews in the school does not fairly represent how many Jews there were in the population. My parents offered some contributions to the building fund for the public high school, hoping that this would help the chances that one of their children would get accepted.

I remember this so clearly: the day I returned from summer vacation and ran excitedly to the high school and looked at the list of incoming freshman girls. My name was not there. I did not get in because, as I was told, the quota for Jews was already filled. The quota was two.

I remember that I was not bitter, just resigned. We were raised, I suppose, to expect and accept this kind of discrimination. I only remember my terrible fear that I might not be able to continue my education. Oh, how we take things for granted now! A high school graduation, then, meant so much!

When my parents heard the news, they then made a decision that forever changed the course of my life. I am sure it was not an easy decision for them—it required they take on a large financial burden. My parents, however, decided to enroll me in a fine, private, commerce high school, one of exceptionally high standards. To this day, I am deeply grateful for the sacrifice my parents made in order to allow me to pursue my education. This opportunity put me in with a very privileged minority of Jewish youth, and was probably one of the most important and determining events of my whole life.

Since I excelled in math, I was happy with the decision that I would be in a school angled toward commerce. "Figures" became a part of my life. I entered the school with a lot of pride, and a feeling of being special. I had had to, of course, pass another entrance exam. You were not accepted in high school just because you were able to pay for it. The fact that parents had to sacrifice to pay for their children's education, beginning at the high school level, was another reason that those who were so lucky to have that chance took their education with a lot more seriousness and pride than kids in our country today.

Our lives in high school were quite controlled—even, some would probably say, regimented. However we did not object nor rebel, nor even disagree, with the standards set for us by our educators. We wore uniforms to school—it was a Catholic school—with our high school emblem embroidered on the left sleeve. For the girls, the uniforms were navy skirts with white blouses, or navy dresses with a white collar. These uniforms were a great treasure to us—we wore them with pride. I am sure such an attitude is difficult for girls these days to imagine, but then again, our uniforms were what showed that we were part of a privileged and intellec-

*With classmates in front of my high school,
spring 1934. I am the third from the left.*

My high school.

tual group. While in high school, we had a strict curfew. We followed it without complaint because we did not want to risk expulsion. The curfew hours were set by the school standards, not by our parents.

The work in school was very difficult and demanding. For privacy, I spent many hours studying in the state park that was so near to us. I loved going there in the very early hours of the morning during spring and fall. I remember clearly the precious, quiet hours of morning, when dew was on the grass, the air was misty, the sky growing light. In those quiet surroundings I would get so absorbed in my studies that some mornings I would forget the time and have to race back home for breakfast at 7:00 am. I never wanted to miss my hot cocoa. Then, it was off to school, which was about a mile walk.

I was a top student throughout my elementary and high school years, and I was always the youngest, usually by two years (I started school a year earlier than most, and I skipped second grade). I remember so little of my actual high school. I don't remember the classrooms—and only vaguely do I recall the large, two-story building and the street it was housed on. I have warm but unclear memories of some classmates and some teachers. My high school years were happy ones. In all my years there, there was only one incident when I felt specifically ostracized and hurt because I was Jewish. It happened when we took our high school graduation portrait in 1939. There were only two Jewish girls in our graduating class. All individual pictures were placed alphabetically, except ours. Our two were on the bottom left side. We were clearly outcasts, set away from others. Even though this shocked and hurt me, I consoled myself with the fact that I had received the highest grades and honors.

Years later, returning to Poland, I went back to my high school to try to recover this group graduation picture. Unfortunately, it could not be found. But I did find the single photo—the only one I have from those times.

My graduation photo, 1939.

I had a very good friend in our school, David Eiger. He was the son of my dad's accountant. (He survived the war and later in his life lived in Minneapolis. We continued our friendship until the day that he died.) Although the boys' classes were housed on a lower floor, David and I often managed to exchange exam information at lunch break. He was a top student in the boys' section. The two of us competed academically, but David always treated me with concern as if I was his little sister. He was very protective. Our parents were very good friends.

I was very well liked by my teachers and never had a problem making friends. I had no problem charming any male teachers, who I think were sometimes more indulgent and lenient with me than they were with others. I had a crush on our German teacher, a young, handsome man. I took German language only because of him, and worked hard to excel above his expectations. I took every class this teacher offered: German Language, German Shorthand, German Business Correspondence, and so on. At the time, I would never have imagined that it would be my knowledge of the German language that, probably helped to save my life during the war. During my visit to Poland forty years later I tried to find this teacher, so that I could tell him how helpful his teachings had been to me during the war years, but he could not be located in school records.

I joined a Zionist youth group named Masada, a co-ed group of elite Jewish high school and university students. The group was started by a few university students. Its purpose was to promote Jewish identity and pride in Radom's Jewish youth and ultimately to raise money to buy land in Palestine (now Israel). I was a member of Masada all four years of high school. It was experience that marked me for a lifetime, and it was deeply important in defining the person I have become. In Masada I made the best friends of my life, had the most fun, studied the hardest, and grew enormously in both confidence and self-knowledge, within the loving group of friends and support that I found there.

Masada was based in the downtown area of the city and it took up a whole floor of an apartment building. There were study rooms, where we often did our homework and where someone was always available if help was needed. There was a ping-pong room, library, auditorium, and gym. Schoolwork was hard and required a lot of time. For those of us that were in Masada, it soon got to be that we spent all our waking hours either in school or at Masada. It became a second home for all of us.

The whole group was a fantastic bunch of kids. We had true, clean fun. There were many adolescent dramas lived through in Masada. There were plenty of love affairs, both happy and less than happy—all accompanied by the usual gossip. I, too, had crushes and flirtations. But throughout my happy time at Masada, I was not serious about anyone.

Fit around all the hard work, study, and regimentation, we spent a lot of effort in charity work and many money-raising projects for Jewish causes. We were very active and always organizing events of one kind or another. Every Friday night we put on an Oneg Shabbat, a celebration welcoming Shabbat, with an almost professional flair. At the local theater we put on musicals featuring the poetry we composed. Our musical director for such events was my best friend Hanka's boyfriend—George Krongold. He was a remarkably talented musician—a professional singer by the age of sixteen, since he had already done radio work.

We worked well in groups—a fact which reflects favorably on the energizing and unifying influence of our two founders: Chaim Kinzler, who now lives in Israel, and Moritz Boyman, now living in Toronto.

Because of my Masada experience, I learned to work well with others and to be at ease and have genuine friendship with both sexes. Also, my time there instilled in me a real love of Zionism and a pride of my heritage. We dreamed, and assumed it could only ever

*Here I am with some of my close friends
from Masada: Marian Meryn, Eva Bar,
and Lilli and George Krongold.*

be a dream, of the creation of a Jewish state. Since I was always with Masada friends, where being Jewish was a source of great pride and rejoicing, I was shielded from exposure to anti-Semitism. My ebulliently optimistic nature and energy flourished in those years.

Late in the '80s I attended an unforgettable three-day reunion of Masada in Israel. It took much planning. A large group of survivors from Masada, and their spouses, arrived from eleven different countries all over the world: the US, Canada, France, Belgium, Sweden, Austria, and even Australia. It is sad how we wound up distributed all over the world.

Masada friends Marian Meryn and George Krongold
are on the right; Maurice Boyman,
one of Masada's founders, is on the left.

Here I am at the Masada reunion with my dear friend
Bella Shore: she's on my far left.

I cannot even begin to describe what joy it was to see so many of my old friends, after forty years, and how sad that so many did not survive. There was so much to reminisce about, so much to rejoice about! We sang songs we used to sing, we traveled throughout Israel—the country we had only dreamed about before. We planted trees for everyone from our group that did not survive. We exchanged stories and addresses and phones numbers to keep in touch.

My husband Marty's memory of his years in Habonim, another youth group, were comparable to mine of Masada. He too developed lasting friendships, and always spoke of those years with much fondness.

My sister belonged to another youth group, our rivals. The main difference I think between her group and ours was that hers had a more radical agenda for land acquisition in Palestine.

School and Masada absorbed my life. The only time I wasn't constantly with my friends from the group was during the summers, when we would go as a family to the cottage that my parents rented in a nearby forest-resort area called Garbatka. Many Radom Jewish families summered there. It was a short train ride from Radom.

The summers were happy, fun times. Garbatka was filled with women and children all week—fathers usually arrived by train on Friday afternoons and would stay for the weekend. We three kids always looked forward to our father's arrival. (Now that I look back on it, I don't remember my father ever taking a vacation. One time I do remember that he and my mother went for a few days to attend a wedding in Warsaw.)

The summers were never boring. I don't know why summer camps in this country have such busy schedules of activities and have to entertain the kids at all times. We only had a radio, but we spent many happy hours just being close to nature, meeting new people, and being close to family. The radio was a gem. We spent many evening hours dancing to the fantastic music from Bucharest, Vienna, or Paris. Those cities were not very far away, and we could pick up the frequency easily.

Some of our family members came occasionally to spend time in our summer cottage. I remember once that my mother was terribly upset with my father's sister who was lazy and took too much advantage of Mom's hospitality. The only arguments I remember my parents having were over Papa's family *schleping* too much from my father in loans or burdening him with many family problems. He was the oldest sibling.

Our maid did not accompany us to our summer cottage, which was small, and Mom was the one who did all the housework. Obviously it was a pretty limited vacation for her. My sister helped, but I seldom did. What a spoiled brat I was! I don't know why they let me get away with it.

As much fun as summer vacations were, I always looked forward to going back to Radom, and to Masada.

I had a very close girlfriend—my darling friend, Hanka Leslau. We became inseparable and were intensely and emotionally close, up until the day that she died. Our friendship was envied. We shared similar traits such as sensitivity, emotionalism, and a penchant for daydreaming—but at the same time both enjoyed the joyous fun of youth. It was a friendship of great love and support and closeness.

My other dearest friend was named Andzia Finkelstein (after the war she became Ann Berman). She was so energetic and bubbly and vivacious! The three of us developed an emotional attachment and shared a level of warmth, devotion, and trust that one does not see frequently. We loved being together, even if we did not have anything to do or anywhere to go. Around the city we soon became known as the "Holy Trio" because we were always together.

My friends loved my mother. They would often stop by our house and were warmly welcomed to join our family for dinner or tea—even if I was not at home! They often asked my mother for advice and confided in her many of their problems.

Hanka came from an extremely wealthy family and they often traveled to Switzerland, Austria, or other European resorts during vacations. We missed each other greatly during her trips. We wrote daily and could hardly wait to be together again.

It was during my time at Masada that I became very close friends with Jurek (George Krongold was his American name). He and my friend Hanka were in love and began dating, despite objections from her parents. Perhaps her family thought him not worthy of her because he came from a more humble background and his financial future was not as secure as they would have hoped for their daughter. They hoped the attachment between George and Hanka would not become too serious. But who could help loving George? He was wonderfully charming, loving, emotional, and passionate about his dreams of making a career in music. He had a great voice and was trained in opera. There was a great love between him and Hanka.

As a good friend to both of them, I was the mediator during their arguments, and both trusted me with the utmost of secrets. George has remained my close friend for a lifetime (sadly, he passed away in 2005). I lost my dear friend Hanka in 1942. But more about this later.

Through the high school years, we Jewish girls mixed socially only with our own kind. The Gentiles had no interest in befriending us. Intermarriage was an infrequent, even an unheard-of, occurrence. Our boyfriends visited the *shiksas* (non-Jewish girls—but the word especially implies girls with loose reputations!) only after they bid us goodnight, for we did not ever go beyond necking.

I would like to point out though that I was never self-conscious about being Jewish in Poland, and, to this day, this segregation problem does not bother me.

Winters were very cold and dry in Poland. Ice skating was the only outdoor sport we could enjoy. For my fifteenth birthday, my last before war broke out, my mother rented a private skating rink for me and my dozen or more friends. It was a great birthday party—so much fun! The rink was very close to our house. There were no separate ice skating shoes available in those days—one simply attached skates to laced, leather shoes.

Some of my friends were excellent skaters. George Krongold was one of these. He seemed to dance on the ice. After we had laughed and skated to our hearts' content, we returned home for hot cocoa and cake. On my return trip to Poland in the late 1980s I went to visit that skating rink, a site of such good memories. It was no longer there but I stood on the spot, emotional, remembering.

We always welcomed the spring. We enjoyed the outdoors tremendously. One of our friends, Helen Silvers, lived on the outskirts of the city, near the brick factory her family owned. She was well off, and often invited us friends out there on Sundays for swimming and picnicking. Her home was five to seven miles away and either we bicycled there or she sent her driver and a horse-drawn carriage to pick us up. We would wait at a specified street corner, and feel very "high class" and enviable as we stepped up into our carriage.

Helen, and her husband Leo Silvers, are my close friends to this day. They live in Florida. We call, we visit, we reminisce. Not over the horrors of war years, but over the beautiful memories of our golden youth.

***

In the summer of 1939 I was looking forward to continuing my pursuit of education in college, but the events in Germany, under Hitler's regime, threw my hopes in doubt. The fear of war and of Hitler's regime was becoming more and more a threat to us. We felt the winds of war. The menace of possible violence oppressed us. We lived with worry from day to day as harrowing news of continuous persecution of German Jews filtered in to us. We got some information from newspapers and from radio, but the most horrifying tales came by word of mouth from refugees that had managed to escape into Poland. We heard that thousands were being jailed and killed in the most abominable, unfathomably awful ways. We were horrified.

The safety and our future plagued and worried our parents. Several prominent people left the city and some even left the country. It was obvious that Poland was going to get invaded. I started pressing my parents to leave. We heard rumors of being able to go to Romania and from there to Palestine. We, the kids, were not as aware of all political news as the current young generation seems to be, but we knew enough to feel uneasy and anxious.

My mother, however, looked around at our home, at our belongings, our history, our friends, our whole life, and said, "How can we leave everything and run?" As she pointed out, all the newspapers and reports were promising that this would be a "blitzkrieg" (a lightning-fast war). No one could imagine that England and America would allow Hitler's takeover of Europe.

Oh! If only I could change this part of our family history! If only we had run when we could have done so by choice—run far away. As it was, soon we would be forced to leave all our possessions behind anyway, when we were compelled to flee into the assigned Jewish area. All my mother's dearly cherished things and memories were left behind, but we had, then, what was important: one another. To this day, I don't get that attached to material things that can be replaced and I don't fall apart about a scratch in the furniture.

Hitler was incredibly effective at influencing German youth. So many people adored him. History books tell us this, but I wouldn't have believed it if it wasn't for an incident that we experienced. Many Jewish children were sent, by their families or charitable organizations, from Germany to Poland—the presumed safe haven. My friend Hanka's parents adopted one of these children, a boy of fourteen. He told harrowing, ghastly stories about what had befallen his family and other Jews, just weeks before, under the Nazi regime. One Friday night I joined them for supper, and the conversation turned to political news. Someone cursed Hitler. The boy, the German Jew—whose own parents had just been sent away to camp—stood up, very insulted, and left the table. We were shocked. And I became convinced that Hitler must have supernatural powers of persuasion and control, over even those he had harmed.

There is no doubt that Hitler had unbelievable power to brainwash millions of followers. There were times when I observed the Germans during Hitler's speech on radio. They would stand upright overpowered and with such a glow in their eyes, filled with such a fascination for Hitler that I thought the man must be unearthly. And the more power he had, the more he was drunk with it, the more he controlled, the more his fury and his appetite for conquest grew. He gave his people a cause and purpose and, whatever the method, most followed him like magic!

Many books were written about the techniques of the Nazis in the slaughter of innocent people in Europe. Not much has been written about the indifference of the Jews to the oppressors. As far as I knew, while in the midst of it, I thought that there was little resistance on the part of the Jews. But I am told, by the historian Sir Martin Gilbert, that actually there was indeed resistance in some ghettos (never in Radom, or I would have heard about it). I am also told, to my surprise, that there was even resistance in the death camp—for example in Treblinka and Sobbibor and in Auschwitz in October 1944 when the Jews blew up the crematorium. There was, of course, the well-known Warsaw uprising, a proud part of the history of the Polish Jews.

I did know, from the beginning stages of the war, about the existence of the "Underground"—the resistance. We had contact with them from the ghetto and from the labor camps in Poland. They helped some to cross over into other countries and escape when possible. I know some of those who did that. I remember also making collections of jewelry and valuables for them.

But the part that used to amaze me was the indifference and the apathy that the world showed, even with the knowledge of Hitler's atrocities. It is hard to believe that those actions that took years for him to carry out could have been so very well concealed that the world was kept in ignorance. Then again, I look at the state of the world now, and hear news of terrible slaughter and suffering committed by one group of people on another, and I know that the pattern of slow, apathetic global movement goes on even today.

And perhaps, regarding our experiences in Europe, how can I blame the world of indifference when we too, in the center of the slaughterhouse, were still so oblivious, and even dismissed the eyewitness reports that trickled in to us. Our stupidity and naiveté shocks me to this day.

The Invasion

It was September 1939 when my world crumbled. Hitler's army invaded Poland.

For weeks prior to the invasion, all the people in our apartment building—Jews and Christians alike—had started preparing for war. We built a shelter, collected food supplies, and even prepared one room into an air-proof shelter in case of gas attacks. As it turned out, the invasion only lasted a laughingly brief five days. We were far over-prepared.

There was some bombing at the beginning and we rushed to the bomb shelter in our backyard several times. I experienced there the first most frightful moments of my life. It was simply terrifying to hear enemy planes overhead and hear the whistle of a bomb falling. Then there would be a split-second wait until you heard the explosion. And then you were so relieved, so thankful, that you were alive to hear it. My heart used to stop during those horrifying seconds. The Germans had no targets; they just terrorized and panicked the people—and it worked. For the first time, I truly prayed—hard—in silent waiting.

On the second or third night of bombing, my parents somehow secured a horse and buggy to take us to a small town where some of my mother's relatives lived. We packed some of our belongings, traveled in the dark of the night, and arrived at dawn at our safe (so we thought) destination. But the invaders played many tricks on us. They found this lovely little town and, for fun, lowered the planes near the ground and machine-gunned dozens of people who were at the marketplace. Then they dropped a few bombs.

I was at the marketplace then. "What a stupid way to fight a war," I thought, even then. One of the explosions threw me about twenty to thirty feet and into a little open grocery store where I fell on a sack of flour and passed out.

A tremendous panic spread immediately through the whole town. My parents at first didn't realize that I was missing, and then they tried desperately to find me. After some hours, they thought I might be dead. When I came to, I found my way home, through the confusion and destruction of the town. The buildings were crumbling and on fire, and people were dying in the streets. I turned up at home all covered with white flour. Mom almost fainted.

After five days of fighting, Nazi tanks roared through our city streets and we were free no longer. The Germans had entered our lives. For most Poles, the hopes and dreams for the immediate future were ended.

Within hours, to my dismay, hundreds of Poles suddenly became part of the German House-Police. They must have been working and spying for the Germans all along. Suddenly, swastika symbols bloomed on their jackets and hats, and they displayed them proudly.

When we returned home we found very little damage done to our city. Recently, I found out (from a friend, who got the information from a German who actually flew the mission over Radom) why our city was spared from excessive bombing. The town of Pionki, very near Radom, housed the biggest ammunition factory and the Germans badly wanted it undamaged.

A human being can be so easily swayed and influenced to behave like an animal. The Polish people put up no fight and practically gave their country away to the Germans, who occupied it within days. And then, how quickly some Poles' attitude toward us Jews became like that of the Germans. Most of them took pride in turning over a Jew to be shot for hiding out, and many Poles participated in all atrocities, even if it was just with silent agreement. I can understand, now, that Jews were Hitler's scapegoats and his "cause" in his ruthless drive for power, but what about the Poles? What explains their behavior? I was born and raised in Poland, and no matter how shielded I was from open acts of anti-Semitism, I did live there and honestly I have to say that the attitude of the Poles, complaisant at best and actively participatory at worst, was no shock to me. It seemed at the time that no one cared. It seemed that we were all doomed. It seemed that there were no decent human beings among the Poles. It was not until many, many years after the war ended that I woke up to the shocking discovery that over five thousand Poles are recognized at *Yad Vashem* for risking their and their families' lives to save Jews. Reading Sir Martin Gilbert's book *The Righteous* opened my eyes to the thousands of unknown heroes of the war.

As the winter of 1939 settled in, the life under occupation became more fearful. The Jews were ordered to wear white armbands with a blue Jewish star so that they could be easily identified. Not wearing one was punishable by death. But, at least in the beginning, we were still in our apartment and Dad still went to his shop, before his factory was confiscated. We managed to get food. Optimistically, we all hoped that this war was going to be a short one and that Germany would be defeated in a matter of months. There were no more schools for the Jews. But, besides having a curfew and wearing an armband, life—for us—continued in a new but semi-normal way. The surrounding tragedies had not had much of a direct impact on us.

But change was upon us. Only three months after the occupation, at the beginning of December 1939, we were forced out of our home. Our area was one of the first to be purged by the Nazis.

They stormed into our apartment in the early morning and gave us one half hour to pack, get out, and move to a designated area. There were no tears, just panic, even though we had all sort of been expecting this. My parents had earlier secured an apartment in the area of the city with a high Jewish concentration. They had arranged that we would share an apartment with a widower friend of my father.

Funny what you think of grabbing first on short notice. My sister dragged her favorite philodendron plant. I threw away my diary, which I had written in for years, because it was not essential. Now, dearly, I regret that loss and I wish I could have hidden it. At the time, though, I thought only to take with me my favorite blue suit and shoes to match. Only my parents worked with a cool head. It is unbelievable how much you can stuff into pillowcases. We left behind, without hesitation, all the accumulation of lovely things that had earlier so pained my parents to part with.

We moved in to my father's friend's apartment, located in the designated Jewish area. We were lucky; my dad's friends welcomed us and tried to make us comfortable. All six of us shared a bit of crowded space. There weren't many tears—just tension and chaos. Nonetheless, we settled in with the hopes that this would surely be temporary and that we could make due. We were still able to move around the city, wearing the armbands with the Jewish star, and we had to adhere to the strict curfew. It was not until about one year later, March 1941, that this area officially became the enclosed ghetto.

My group of friends stuck together. There was nothing to do but try to amuse ourselves. There were eight of us—four couples. There was Hanka Leslau and George Krongold. The recent political turmoil had only made their love more strong and sure. And there was Bella Shore, Isydor Boyman, Moniek Sylberberg and Moniek Meryn. The last two people in this tight circle of friends were Andzia and I—neither of us were in love or were interested in anyone beyond the level of flirtation.

We spent days and evenings together, mainly at the home of Isydor Boyman (who, after the war, moved to Paris) because it was close and convenient. We played cards, read, danced, listened to music on the radio, and literally spent hundreds of hours listening to opera records. None of us, besides George Krongold, had any love or understanding for opera at first, but George was a singer, so he taught, explained, and instilled in us the love for opera and classical music. We would lie on the floor in a dimmed room at Isydor's apartment and forget the world—we were absorbed in the beauty of music. I learned to dream with music, imagine my own visual scenarios of many wonderful things, create many wishful and fanciful visions. I still love to indulge in daydreams. It takes me away from reality and I can bask in an untroubled fantasy world, temporarily. Sometimes we got so lost in the music that we would stay past curfew and have to spend the night.

Funny how many times I think back to those months of occupation as the most beautiful ones in my life. It might sound strange, given the circumstances surrounding us, but we really felt quite carefree—we could not, after all, change the political condition (and we always thought it would be over soon) and also we were so very much wrapped up in ourselves that we did not care much about the world outside our little sanctuary.

We were normal, healthy kids with normal desires, but we never crossed the border of clean fun and wonderful, uncompromised friendship.

George—or Jurek as we called him—was a gem in those long days and evenings of the early months of the war. He sang and played guitar endlessly, and was so much fun to listen to. He boldly hid his guitar under a topcoat and managed to smuggle it to Isydor's house.

Since George's uncle was a physician, head of a hospital in Radom, and his three brothers were also physicians, they arranged for George to have a pass so that, as a "physician's assistant," he was able to move around more freely than most after curfew hours. The city was not an easy place to travel after dark. German soldiers were everywhere—it was frightening. My mother was ill with a mastoid infection that was very dangerous and George, having acquired a bit of medical knowledge from his family, would come every six hours around the clock, even during the dangerous night hours, to change my mother's complicated compresses.

There was one incident that temporarily shook us up. George was singing an opera and it must have been loud enough to penetrate the closed windows and the walls of the apartment. Suddenly, there was a knock on the door and a German officer appeared.

"Who was singing?" he asked.

George, with fear in his eyes, stood up, prepared to be punished for disturbing the peace.

"May I shake your hand?" asked the officer. "You have a magnificent voice. I am a member of the Berlin Opera, and I would love to work with you and give you advice, for such talent such as yours is rare."

After that, George met him and they developed a rare friendship, under those circumstances.

George survived the war on Christian papers in Warsaw, and married his wife, Lili, there. He was "discovered" after the war ended, and was the protégé of a famous opera singer, Benjamino Gigli. He sponsored George to study opera in Milan, Italy. George and Lili spent several years after the war there, all expenses paid. But he decided to come to the US and join the surviving members of his family, foolishly thinking that he would surely "make it" here. He never did.

I am sure that the wonderful experience of my friendship with this close circle of friends contributed to my ability to endure the war. The happiness I felt, and the great affirmation and encouragement I had from them, gave me confidence and optimism, and also a conviction of the potential good and beauty of people. These were qualities that helped me survive, and they influenced the course of my life ever after.

During those months, I volunteered in the temporary setup of the Jewish Community Center office and in the Health Center. I kept as busy as possible. And, except for the curfew, I felt still relatively free and at ease moving around my city.

Just for fun, I started eyeing a certain boy. He was always surrounded with girls, and paid very little attention to me. Moniek Horowicz was tall, very handsome, and very popular. But I didn't give up easily. The challenge intrigued me. I saw him from time to time and would try to run into him, but he continued not to show me any special attention. Then, one morning, he smiled and waved at me. Well, that was enough joy to last me for days.

Soon I figured out where and when he passed on certain days. I never missed a day to "accidentally" be there—and I usually dragged Andzia and Hanka along with me. It didn't matter that I saw him almost each time with another girl. I was powerfully attracted to him.

One morning, I looked out the window of our apartment, and who should I see coming out of the building—the one I had just moved into—but *him*, my dream boyfriend! Moniek Horowicz. I was absolutely breathless. It would seem that *he* lived here too! I couldn't believe it!

I could not fall asleep that night. I stayed awake until I saw him return late from what I presumed must have been yet another date. (With a little pull you could still obtain an evening pass.) A few days later I managed an "accidental" run-in, and for the first time, we sat on a bench in the yard and talked.

That was the beginning of a most beautiful and unusual friendship, one that lasted not only through the war but was remembered and cherished by both of us throughout our adult years.

We spent many, many evenings together, alone, talking for hours. He acted at times as a father, a teacher, a friend, and a boyfriend. Moniek always treated me with the utmost of tenderness and affection. We spent time discovering each other's feelings, hopes, and dreams. Although he was two or three years older than me, he still confided in me his problems and his joys, and listened to my suggestions. We talked about the future, the present, and the past. I was, despite my age, a very naive girl when it came to sexual matters. I remember how he laughed when he kissed me on my mouth for the first time. He taught me more about life than anyone ever before.

Moniek, though, was a spoiled boy—he always had many girls that loved him. He knew that he was a wonderful lover, and he knew he had absolutely no makings of a husband-to-be. Moniek warned me of this and repeated it often. "Maniunia," he would say, "please don't fall in love with me. You deserve better." We loved being together, and we looked forward to the evenings spent in the garden of the building. The building we lived in had a great yard, so we did not have to worry about a curfew. Moniek's parents owned the building and, one night, their gardener graciously offered us the use of his apartment in the garden, so we could be comfortably alone. The gardener absolutely did not believe that I was still a virgin, after all that. We laughed and laughed about it.

I truly grew up during those months. I matured sexually, mentally, and physically.

Years later, I wondered how my mother felt about this relationship. Did she disapprove of my spending so much time alone with him? Or was she glad that I had fun despite the ominous gloom that permeated the rest of our world? She never criticized me, never showed any anxiety, nor asked any questions. At that point, anyway, I was too engrossed in my little world for my mother's feelings to matter very much to me. I was so in love it hardly even mattered to me what was happening at home or, to a certain extent, in the outside world.

I remember that year's festival of Rosh Hashanah and Yom Kippur. A small group of Jews from the building gathered at Moniek's house for prayers. There was no rabbi and no cantor to chant the prayers, and my thoughts went back to years past when we were kids and played in the yard of the synagogue during the services. The air around us would fill with the chanting and such an intensity of feeling that, to this day, cantorial music fills my eyes and ears with melancholy. But the prayers were quiet that year and there was a lot to pray for. I watched our fathers' heads covered with prayer shawls, swaying occasionally, and I said a quiet prayer in my own words, pleading that there would be an end to the suffering the war had brought us. I prayed by offering, by vowing a small sacrifice, entreating to be listened to.

And yet, despite the solemnity we knew was real, we kids still could not help being somewhat lighthearted. I remember on that Yom Kippur day we started fasting, as usual, but by noon Moniek and I sneaked out for lunch at a friend's restaurant. We couldn't take worries about tomorrow too seriously. After all, we thought, the war would surely end soon.

The Ghetto

The ghetto area was created in spring of 1941. It was surrounded with barbed wire. The Nazis had pushed us into a small area so that they would have easy access to us. The only connection to

Entrance to the Radom ghetto.

the outside world was through a gate that was guarded by the German police twenty-four hours a day. It was announced through a loudspeaker and on posted notices that anyone leaving without permission would be killed instantly. A Jewish council was formed to administer the ghetto. They handled the distribution of food rations and medical supplies.

I still saw my close friends often. Of course now we were living closer than ever. We were one another's lifelines during this time of chaos. I think my friends helped me keep my positive outlook.

During the last few months, while we lived in Moniek's family's building, I started working for a German outfit.

It was the energetic Andzia who arranged it—or perhaps it was her mother, who was an aggressive lady. Andzia convinced me to do it because, she said, working for the Germans would help keep me safe. We were picked up for work in a truck, and then taken outside the ghetto to perform various odd jobs. The one I was assigned to do first was to clean offices at the German army officers' quarters.

Well, I am ashamed to admit it, but up to that time, I had never cleaned house before. I had no idea how. But, I tried. I found myself alone in a room, and I started wiping surfaces, hoping that this was how one dusted. In the midst of my efforts, a German officer entered the room. He watched me for a moment, and then started laughing! "You've never done this before, have you?" he asked me. Now you'd think I would have been terrified to have this Nazi officer speak to me—anything might have happened. But I didn't know what else to do but be honest. "It's true," I told him, in my schooled German. "I don't know what I am doing."

The officer then proceeded to show me how to clean! First, we made up the bed. Then, we cleared everything from the desk and dusted it, and so on. He cleaned his own room, good-naturedly.

Shortly after that I was transferred from maid duty to the job of washing windows in an empty building. Thank God I was working alongside my friends, because I had no idea how to wash windows either, but they did theirs, then helped teach me. This was the first time I'd ever heard that windows are cleaned best with paper!

The German *Wehrmacht* (drafted soldiers) in this particular outfit treated us with courtesy and some kindness, but they never crossed the line and became friendly—or, for that matter, anything sinister. An interesting and unique result of the German conviction of their superiority over Jews was that they would never consider having anything to do, physically, with a Jewish girl. That would have been considered dirtying to German purity, and they may have risked instant death. We girls, otherwise so vulnerable, were safe in that regard.

Andzia and Hanka and I worked together. The holy trio remained intact. I was transferred from one job to another, until eventually the Germans decided that they'd get the most work out of me if I was at a desk, so I wound up in an office. Happily, Andzia and Hanka also obtained similar jobs, and it was because all three of us spoke German.

My knowledge of the German language came in extremely handy. My boss was a middle-aged German army man with the last name of Baker. He was, without doubt, a warm and caring person. He was patient while teaching me office procedures, and gently corrected my German and my typing errors. Mr. Baker shared his lunches with us, and the food parcels he received from home in Berlin. This kind of generosity was, of course, forbidden. Mr. Baker called us "Mine Kinder"—my children.

I considered Mr. Baker a dear friend. Later, this man would actively save my life. It is little wonder that he will always have a special place in my thoughts and prayers. To this day, I resent that the persecution of the Jewish people in the '40s is attributed to the "Germans," without specifying that it was the *Nazi* Germans who were responsible. There was a great difference between the members of the Nazi Party—true adherents to the Nazi doctrine and willing participants in the Nazi tactics—and those Germans who were simply drafted army men, many of them aged forty or fifty, who were caught up in their country's insane policies.

The father of one of my friends was able to arrange for a Polish passport to be forged in my name and some in the names of several of my friends. A few of my friends escaped to other cities, posing as Christians. I did not hesitate to discuss the idea with Mr. Baker, my German boss. He was strongly in favor—he enthusiastically advised me to take advantage of this opportunity to escape, and he even offered counsel on where it was best to go and how to behave in order to not be detected. He tried very hard to convince me that there was nothing but terrible, dark times ahead for Polish Jews.

Much as I respected his advice, I simply could not bring myself to consider leaving my family, even if it was to save my own life, as he insisted. At this point, even though we lived in a closed ghetto, life was still bearable and, optimistically, I maintained faith that life would soon improve. I don't know what gave me this optimism. Perhaps it was cowardliness that made me accept the circumstances and not want to fight. Or maybe it was naiveté. I'd had a life so blessed with good fortune and times of happiness, I simply couldn't conceive of the hellish circumstances that Mr. Baker hinted at.

Our dear Christian-Polish friends and ex-neighbors, Mr. and Mrs. Kubicka, did not forget us nor desert us. They arranged for a pass that allowed my sister to work in their shop. And most every day, Mrs. Kubicka would send her back with a little extra food for us. She would find ways to hide it on Rella's body, undetectable to the Nazi police, so that Rella could smuggle it in. Still, it was taking one hell of a chance—if found, she would have been shot on the spot.

In 1945 when Rella was able to return to Poland after the war ended, the Kubickas embraced her as if she was their own child coming back to see them. The love and care they showed to our family was very untypical of the feelings most Christian Poles had towards Jews at the time.

The Kubickas tried to help us in many other ways as well. They owned a hat shop and also a bottling plant outside the city limits, and offered to hide my mother on their factory property. My mother, we worried, was the most vulnerable during these troubled times because she was older—so the Nazis might consider her invaluable, and therefore dispensable—and she didn't have any work papers to secure her elsewhere. (Though my father was older too, he did not run the same risk. Being a man, he would always be deemed an essential worker.) The Kubickas thought that she would be safe hiding on their grounds. But Mother did not want to leave us. We stayed together, the whole family, in the ghetto.

Meanwhile, life in the ghetto became increasingly worse and more dangerous. Food rations were drastically reduced. Random raids on the ghetto streets increased in frequency and brutality; people were picked off the streets and disappeared, never to be heard from again.

We heard more and more terrifying news about German victories. I remember feeling fear and uncertainty. I would look at my parents' worried faces and get no response. Even though many in the community still adopted an attitude of denial and tried to ignore the bad news, the rumors of Germans' actions against the Jews continued to trickle in, and we wondered and worried. A growing sense of unease and anxiety permeated the city. It was impossible to identify exactly why we had a growing sense of dread, but everyone felt it. When, one night, the Germans installed bright lights in the center of town, whispers flew around of impending trouble.

Deportations

August 5, 1942. That afternoon Hanka and I were walking home from our work at the Wehrmacht office. We got to the corner where we usually parted ways. She turned to me, and her eyes searched my face with an unsettling intensity. "Kiss me. I have a strange feeling that I'll never see you again," she said. She looked at me a long time—her gaze so penetrating, like she was memorizing my image forever. The only time I have ever seen a look like that was when, twenty-eight years later, I visited my boyfriend, Moniek and he gazed at me at our parting, in this same strange way. (Shortly afterwards, he died unexpectedly.) I don't remember how I responded to Hanka that evening. I am sure I hugged her tightly, and told her to dispel such thoughts from her head—*of course* she would see me again.

Hanka was deported that night. This was the first *oussiedlung* (deportation) from the ghetto. She and her mother were pushed into a train, in the dark of night. She probably never knew that her destination, where she was about to die, was the gas chambers of Treblinka. This is where, also, my mother and little brother were to perish, quite soon thereafter.

When I found out what had happened, I truly cannot describe my grief. In fact, friends and family refrained from telling me, for days, about her disappearance and possible death. They feared for my sanity. And with good cause. This was the first instance that someone close to me—she was closer than a sister—was torn away from me. I had never yet grieved as hard as I did for her then. I was wholly unprepared. I was devastated. With Hanka's death, a part of me also died, and I was never the same. I became more frightened and unsure of my own safety.

I would not be alive today if not for Mr. Baker. He knew about the first *oussiedlung* and he found out what day the second train trip was scheduled for. Without any explanations, he ordered us girls to go home, pack a few belongings and valuables, and then to return to work immediately. To the chain of command above him he claimed that he had emergency work orders at early morning hours, and so he was ordering us to stay at work for the night.

I went home. But I had an ominous premonition about what this strange work order might imply, and I decided to defy the order, and stay home with my family. My mom pleaded with me to leave. I'll never forget her words. "I have lived my life. You are so young—save yours if you can." (At the time, she was in her early forties.) I refused to leave. "I am staying, Mama, we will all stay together."

Back at the office my friend Andzia realized that I was not returning and became frantic. She bribed one of the guards with her watch, as she told me when I asked her about it forty years later. He came to the ghetto, to our apartment, and forced me to get out. I looked at my family. Shaking, I started my goodbyes. How can I describe the fear, the worry, and the agony of leaving them? My heart was very heavy when finally I went out the door.

We stayed overnight in a deserted warehouse—all thirty of us girls. Mr. Baker stood outside all night with a shotgun in his hand, guarding our safety. We *kibitzed* and teased him about his over-concern. Little did we know that he had practically stolen us, without any permission to do so from the higher officers.

At about 5:00 a.m. we started hearing shots. Our first instinct was to run back home to our families, but Mr. Baker forced us to stay in, and to be silent.

The unforgettable day of August 15, 1942.

Thousands were killed that night, or taken by train to the gas chambers of Treblinka. Memories from that night of horror return often to me in my dreams.

The details of the night reached us by morning. My mother and my thirteen-year-old brother had been taken away. I was frantic and I feared that they would never return.

Andzia and her mother, who was with her, did everything in their power to ease my sorrow. Andzia even slept with me so that I could constantly feel her presence, her love for me, her deep concern.

My sister's life had been miraculously saved by two of my dear friends who had been working in the city as Jewish police aides. One of them was Marian Meryn and the other was Leon Bergeisen. Leon recognized her during the confusion and signaled to the other who, pretending that my sister was his wife, was permitted to pull her to safety. This was a lie that would have been punishable by death. My dear friend Marian Meryn, who now lives in Vienna, always asks about my sister in our conversations. We always remember that night.

My father had been passed over during the raid because he had some sort of papers. I cannot even imagine how awful it must have been for him to be a witness as his wife and son were torn away.

***

Mr. Baker. He was a brave, wonderful German soldier who probably risked his career, and possibly much more, to hide and save this group of Jewish girls. I thought many times, after the war ended, to try to find him and feel guilty to this day for not pursuing it. I discussed this topic with Andzia. She thought that he would be scared to "surface." There were enough Nazis left in Germany, even decades after the war, to cause great harm to those who had been good to Jews.

After the war ended people did not talk about rescuers. I don't know why, but no one wrote or talked about it. Even when they built the Holocaust Memorial Center in West Bloomfield they refused at first to assign a part of it to the rescuers who risked their lives to save others. I am glad that the story of Herr Baker, my rescuer, is in Sir Martin Gilbert's book, *The Righteous*.

Mr. Baker was exceptional, but there were other Germans whom we were in contact with while working in Radom, Wsola, and later in Pionki, who were warm and helpful and seemed empathetic about our situation. Even much later while in Germany in concentration camps, we encountered many incidents of concerned German civilians, especially women, who openly showed contempt for the country's regime. For some reason, most survivors hesitate to admit it. We rarely acknowledge that a full half of the German population did not join the Nazi Party, and that half was sometimes a visible and felt presence.

***

For a little while, we girls remained at work, living in the ghetto.

As we realized more and more the extent to which the Nazis would go, many people did everything they could to flee from the ghetto. Most of the people went to Warsaw, the capital of Poland, on Christian papers. Warsaw was a big city and it was easy to get lost in the crowd. Sadly, even there it was not always safe though. My friend Bella was almost caught, but somehow she escaped and eventually wound up in Denmark. She stayed in Denmark, married, then divorced and came to the US some twenty years later. She attended graduate school at the University of Michigan, and she struggled financially. Through all this time, we did not know that we were so close to one another. Someone recognized her in New York, years later, and we were reunited.

Wsola, Poland–
Summer 1942

I don't remember how soon after that terrible night of deportation I was sent to Wsola, a labor camp, on a spacious farm near Radom. It was quick, forced, and I didn't have much to take with me after living in the ghetto. I never had a chance to say goodbye to my family or to Moniek, my love.

Given the alternatives (which, at the time, I did not even fully know about), Wsola was a miraculously good place to be. I was given an office job (my knowledge of the German language paid off again). Our location was in the countryside, away from the stress and fear of the ghetto, and we had livable conditions. My work was easy and clean, and the food was acceptable. I am sure that Mr. Baker must have been responsible for arranging this for us, and for recommending me to an office job. He actually came and visited several times while we were there on the farm. I was even given reassurance that the safety of my father and sister—who were still trapped in the ghetto—had been secured temporarily. I can only think it was his intervention.

My father was going almost insane with grief and worry over my mother and brother. He paid a lot of money to influential people to try and find them. He turned to religion like a fanatic, which, I am sure, saved his sanity.

One of the people my father turned to for help to find my mother and my brother was Kubicka's son-in-law, Krysia's husband. He worked for a high-echelon German outfit and had connections. Finding out the truth about the gas chambers but not wanting, or being able, to reveal it, this young man tried to convince Dad to abandon the search. I remember Dad getting very angry at him, and the whole Kubicka family, after that.

We all truly hoped that our loved ones who were sent away were still alive. Stupid stories circulated that all those abducted had been sent out to the Russian front to work. We believed these stories. The alternative was too terrible to consider.

My mother and my brother had both had a small fortune sewn into their clothing. Each one of us had some valuables hidden for emergencies. I had several gold coins hidden in the heels of the shoes I that wore all the time—a great pair of sturdy shoes, made especially to last a very long time. This was one of many mistakes my father made. The shoes were too nice. Eventually—when I arrived in Auschwitz—a German woman noticed them and took them away from me.

There were many clever ways people smuggled jewelry or money, besides burying it in the ground. Some women carried jewelry in their vaginas. Some people had dentists insert diamonds into fillings.

My sister and I lived through the war with no jewels, no money. The only legacy our parents left us can not be measured in monetary value.

I felt safe in Wsola. And, since my office job gave me a little influence with the German soldiers who ran the camp, I managed to get my sister, and her husband, into our camp. She had married her childhood sweetheart while we were living in the ghetto. My father remained in the ghetto. Those of my friends who still remained there visited him often. Frequently they brought him food, cigarettes, and, most of all, a little cheer and hope. His sister, Pesa, was there too so he was not all alone.

My friends often sent us packages of goodies from the ghetto. They found ways.

I did not see my boyfriend Moniek for weeks. From the moment I arrived Wsola, I could not get him out of my mind. Finally, I managed to persuade my bosses in the office to allow me a short visit to the ghetto. I had a pass for several hours.

First, I went to visit my father. How he had changed! He had lost weight. He looked frail and was obviously very depressed. We had very little time together.

Then, I went to see Moniek. I felt sure that this would be our last goodbye. I knew that I could never have him just for myself anyway, but I needed that goodbye. I needed a last embrace. We had a beautiful, unforgettable moment together, Moniek and I. It was romantic, and emotional, and we shared, to the greatest extent that we could, our love and tenderness for one another.

I returned to Wsola teary-eyed, and feeling like a changed person.

***

But when you are young and full of imagination, you find optimism and cheer no matter what the circumstances. You bounce back quickly.

There were about seventy-five to a hundred of us there in Wsola, young adults and kids. This location was considered a privileged work camp, and indeed it was. We had some freedom and control over our lives. When my sister and I found an abandoned chicken coop on the premises I asked for permission that we might occupy it. It was granted, and we went to work rebuilding that into our own private living quarters. We scrubbed it clean, and then made quite a palace out of it with bunk beds and even curtains in the window which gave privacy for the two married couples (we invited our friends Renia Mandelbaum, who lived in Tel Aviv after the war, and her husband and sister to live with us). It was the privacy that was especially precious. The rest of the workers lived in large barracks. When I returned to visit Poland in 1979 I was tempted to go see Wsola and visit our chicken coop. But I was too afraid of painful memories, and did not.

And so, the war progressed. We were not confined, but were free to move around the farm. The work was easy, and we had good food. The German boss was a grouch, but the rest of the German guards were bearable and some were even very friendly. We lived without fear and we enjoyed laughter and hope and optimism. I managed to hang on to these good sentiments and encouraging feelings for most of the war. But the war provided a steady steam of slowly worsening situations. Every change was to a situation worse than the one previous. Perhaps this slow progression was a good thing because our minds and bodies had time to adjust to the deteriorating circumstances. Maybe that helped us survive. In retrospect, Wsola is a place of, funny as it may sound, pleasant memories. Or is it that I tried hard to forget many unpleasant incidents?

There was one event that gave me chills. The ghetto experienced another *oussiedlung* (deportation to gas chambers). There were several people—mostly family members of people already in Wsola—who managed to escape that night from the ghetto and arrived in our "sanctuary." During the head count the next morning (I don't know why, but they counted us forever), the Germans discovered that there were extra people in the crowd. All hell broke loose and the head of our camp announced that he was going to return the extra people to the ghetto, which of course meant certain death for them.

It was known around camp that, for a bottle of whiskey, we could buy little favors from our German boss. As a result, he was often drunk and wild in behavior. Now, someone had a bottle of whiskey and, since I worked in the office, I was chosen to do the bribing.

I remember shaking. I had never dealt with such circumstances before. My usual way of being was just naive and straightforward, but I knew that now I could not just hand the bottle to him. When on my mission, I put the bottle into the drawer of his desk while he was out of the office. With my heart pounding and my legs shaking, I later stepped into his office. I summoned all my strength and composure, and quietly started to plead for the kids who had escaped the ghetto and infiltrated our numbers. Carefully, I tried to convince him that he needn't report the extra heads because we could share the same amount of appropriated food—and at the same time we could accomplish a lot more work and more quickly, and this would certainly please his superiors. (Remember, I spoke German well).

"But, how will we handle the job assignments on the books?" he asked.

"Well, this is my job," I said. "I will be responsible and I will not endanger your position.

It was after he had agreed to this arrangement that I smiled and shakily told him that I had left something in his desk drawer, a little gift which had been smuggled out of the ghetto. He was full of smiles when he saw it, and I was mighty proud of myself for having accomplished such an enormously difficult task, which, for him, was just a plain favor.

After the war I nearly forgot this whole incident until one of the boys who lived through the war looked me up and could not thank me enough for saving his life, as he put it.

The "good times" in Wsola, however, lasted only a few months. Change was soon upon us. Only weeks after the incident with my boss, quite unexpectedly, several trucks arrived on our farm and it was announced that we were going to be transferred.

I remember being in the office at the time and not knowing what to do. I had not been told to leave. My mind raced. I wondered what would happen if I just sat quietly now, and if they forgot to take me. But then, my boss, with an apology, asked me to leave with the others. At the time I was typing something out, and I purposefully didn't finish the sentence. I hoped that my abrupt ending would be noticed by Mr. Baker, and that this would signal to him that we had been moved. I hoped he would take care of me and my family again. Little did I know at the time that he had already done so. It was he who was arranged this transfer to an even more safe and secluded area.

Pionki, Poland

Pionki is a small Polish town, about fifty or sixty miles from Radom, known mostly because the largest ammunition factory in Poland was located there. The factory was hidden in a thick forest and therefore protected from possible air attacks. The factory, as far as I know, is still in existence today. This was our destination, and it was soon to become our home for the next year and a half.

We arrived in the labor camp of Pionki filled with uneasiness and anxiety.

The Germans needed the factory very badly and quickly staffed it with several hundred young Jewish girls and boys. Our group became part of this labor force. A camp was set up nearby for our living quarters. An inside camp administration was quickly organized. After only a few weeks of my ineffective labor on the factory floor, I was transferred to work in the camp administration office inside the compound.

We started this new phase of our life with a lot of apprehension, of course, but when we realized that our living conditions again were bearable, we were all childishly—perhaps foolishly—optimistic. We presumed that this was the worst of it, that we would wait out this *blitz-krieg* (lightning war) in our new sanctuary, waiting for it to end, presumably soon.

Although our movements were restricted to the compound (there was a fence around it), we could move around within almost as we pleased. It was spacious, and in a very pretty forest setting. No one bothered us, and there seldom was inspection. The food was fair. Some people worked hard, some had it easier, depending on the assigned job. We were treated strictly, but without cruelty.

I again managed to secure separate living quarters for my sister, her husband, and myself.

I remember little of my time spent at Pionki. Life went on. We made the best of the circumstances. My work was easy and pleasant. We met many new people who were also transferred. I made many new friends.

Although my sister and I had been much estranged from one another as children, our feelings had altered completely. We had become close and trusting. My sister embraced me with a motherly love that no one else could have matched. Our new feelings of closeness and attachments remained unchanged to this day.

We often got word from the ghetto and from our father that all was okay. I remember receiving little surprise packages from my friends from the ghetto: cigarettes, candy, toilet soap, etc.

My friend Andzia and I were in the camp together. We were as close as ever. The holy trio was down to two. We sent word that this place was a heaven compared with life in the ghetto. In Pionki, girls met boys, there were love affairs, sex, jealousy—these were everyday preoccupations that allowed our lives to feel almost normal. A clinic was set up in our compound. There were two doctors, and I think they were busy performing abortions.

I met a boy I cared about at the time and Andzia did too. Our guys were pretty influential in the administration and we were proud of it. There were no secrets between Andzia and me and we were as close as twins.

My sister and I decided that it would be best to bring our dad to be with us and we managed to accomplish this. He was thin, had lost even more weight, but otherwise he insisted that he felt fine. We were thrilled to be together—what was left of our family.

We got used to life in Pionki and we were positive that we would be there until the war ended. Which, surely, would be soon.

The camp's work force of several hundred laborers was divided into groups and marched to work under the watchful eye of the German or Jewish guards assigned to it. We were not permitted to leave campgrounds unguarded. There were three of us working in the camp office with one head man and one camp director. My father was assigned to normal physical factory labor, but in his weakened condition, he could hardly bear it. I begged my superiors for a favor to transfer my father to easier work. Weeks went by and nothing was done.

I was honestly ashamed to have it so easy, and felt helpless when I saw him so exhausted at night, after a twelve-hour day's work. I began fearing for his health— and for his life, because I knew enough now to know that the Germans would not spare useless people.

One day, I decided to do the only thing that I thought might improve my father's situation. Without telling my sister or anyone else, I resolved to go straight to the head of the factory and ask him for the favor of changing my father's job.

That morning, I picked up a folder from the office files, and with all the courage I could muster, walked confidently up to the gate and asked to be escorted to the head office immediately, since I had important papers to be signed. I had never seen the head man of our factory and as the guard walked me through the factory and several offices, I could feel my heart pounding like a hammer. I didn't have a plan—just a flicker of hope— and this hope seemed very faint when I finally found myself in front of the door to the office of the president. His name was Herr Brendt.

I was presented as carrying important papers from camp office, and for the first time I looked into the eyes of the man everyone feared so much. He was my father's age, graying, stout, and with a stern expression. There was a young German secretary sitting at his desk holding a steno book.

He turned to me and said impatiently, "What is it that you need me so urgently for? Give me the papers."

I looked directly into his eyes and said, without any trembling in my voice, "I am not here on camp business. It's personal. May I talk to you alone?"

He was so startled that for a moment he said nothing, but then he turned to the secretary and the guard who had brought me and ordered them out.

He asked me to sit down (unheard of! He probably thought I was going to faint).

I started then, in my near-perfect German, by telling him how it hurts me to see my father work so hard. I assured him that he could manage fine but, I said, "I don't know if you have a daughter my age or not, but if you do, you will understand my intentions. She would do the same for you. Please, change his job."

Herr Brendt looked at me for a long time. I can't remember any German's face as well as I do the face of this man. It began to mellow. His expression gradually transformed to one of such compassion, it is impossible that I'll ever forget it. When he finally spoke, his words exceeded my hopes.

"What is your father's name? Where is he working now? What kind of work would your father like to do?" he asked.

There was one job in Pionki that was a godsend. It was to be the repairman whenever a machine broke down. Mostly, the two or three men assigned this work spent the day just sitting in a room, playing cards usually, while waiting for the phone to ring to summon them to do a repair.

I explained to the head of the camp that my father had owned and run a factory, he knew how to repair machines, and that he would be perfect for this job.

Herr Brendt called the guard and told him to take me back to camp.

Before I had even arrived back at the camp, my legs weak after the stress of what I had just done, a special guard had already been sent to pick up my father and take him to his new job.

My family and most of all my office superiors did not believe my story when I explained what had happened. They insisted to know who I had bribed, and how much. Even now many people have a hard time believing the exchange I had with Herr Brendt.

With my father in his new position, my spirits were greatly lifted. Life in Pionki continued in a normal sort of way, though there were some very tragic moments that shocked us and reminded us that we were not free, that we were under forced encampment under German administration.

One time, one of the kids was hanged. I don't remember what "crime" it was that he committed—perhaps he smuggled something into camp. We were forced to watch the hanging. Anyone that put their heads down or closed their eyes was beaten. The boy died calling out the Hebrew words, "Long live freedom, God be with you!"

Another day a brother of one of our friends in camp arrived after a miraculous escape from the gas chambers of Treblinka. In the evening he gathered a group of us and accounted with detail the train trip, the harrowing story of the arrival, the gassing of the people in masses, and how he had been chosen with five others to sort the clothing of the dead. The boys had then escaped by throwing handfuls of sand into the eyes of the guard watching them, and then running and running. Only two of the six of them had made it.

When he told us his story, we were incredulous. We thought he was lying, or had lost his mind. We simply could not believe it. The incident, the whole story, was quickly forgotten.

I want to tell you an interesting story with a happy ending. Among the hundreds of workers in the camp, there was a little girl in our compound. She was five or six, the daughter of the Kaplans from Radom. I am sure it was not legal for a child to be there. There were no other children in our compound, but she was so smart and knew how to hide during threatening situations. Later she told me that at times it was live or die. I lost track of that family but saw them briefly two years later at my wedding ceremony.

In the late 1980s I visited my daughter Joani in LA. We were shopping and, tired, I decided to rest in the shoe department while waiting for Joani to finish. A young woman watched me for a while, walked around me, studying my face. I was puzzled.

Finally she approached me and asked, "May I ask you a question? Were you in Pionki?" "Yes," I replied.

"Are you Mania?"

"Yes . . ."

"I am Tobie Kaplan," she said.

It was her, the little girl from the camp! We had watched over her and tried to keep her safe. She had recognized me after all those years probably because I was a somewhat visible presence, one of the few who worked in the front office.

What a reunion that was! What a joy it was to see

her alive and well and all grown up.

***

During the fall and winter, I was glad to work in a warm office in Pionki. News of the US joining the allied forces reached us, and new hope entered our hearts. We saw that the Germans had begun to have problems. Men up to the age of about fifty or older were being drafted. Food supplies were getting worse. We felt and saw the disorder and some anxiety among the Germans. We overheard their conversations, and bits from the radio, and we knew that the Russian front was advancing. We hoped that the end was near, but at the same time we feared what changes the Germans would resort to as their situation worsened. Above all, we feared getting transferred. A transfer, we suspected, would mean a worse situation.

We would have been content to have stayed and worked at Pionki until the war ended, but Hitler had different plans for us in mind. It was spring of 1944 when our peaceful existence was threatened. Indeed, as we had feared, a notice came to us one day stating the date that the camp was closing and that we would be transferred. We received word from Herr Brendt, our Pionki factory head, who was in touch with Herr Baker, our savior, that our destination would be Czechoslovakia and the camp Theresienstadt.

Any transfer was worrisome, but by nature I had great faith that any situation could be bearable if you had the right attitude. I was always optimistic and, of course, I was wholly convinced that I had been born lucky, so things were destined to always work out, somehow. This attitude of optimism helped keep me going through these months and years of forced labor and made life bearable. In fact, I used to spread cheer and hope among all around me, friends and strangers alike, and try to lift their spirits. Sometimes now, when I get depressed and so discouraged, I wonder if I am the same person of so very, very long ago. Then, I guess I had the strength of youth. I was determined not to give in and my aim throughout the war, to the bitter end, was to live through it all, no matter what.

We had heard rumors of an underground organization of Polish fighters who accepted Jews. Although we were under guard, escape from Pionki was not difficult; we were surrounded by forests. When news of the upcoming transfer came to us, some did make the break, but only very few did it. I was tempted too but was torn and couldn't decide. I was afraid of forcing change, of stepping out into the unknown on my own.

The camp director ordered a dozen people to remain in Pionki in order to do the office closing procedures and cleanup jobs. Because I was working in the office, I was one of the few chosen to stay behind. It meant not going with the masses to another camp; it meant perhaps a life-saving situation. This presented me a very painful situation. I thought about my father and my sister and her husband, who looked up to me always for help, with an aching heart. The decision to stay or to go weighed heavily on my mind for days.

I never told them, nor asked for advice about what to do. I spent many hours conversing with myself, and with God. Eventually I realized that I just could not desert them. If I stayed and they left, I could not live with myself.

And so, without regret, on a cold morning, I joined all the others in climbing into a freight train where we were packed tight as sardines.

I remember being so frightened. I prayed so hard, and I felt God's presence and hope, and strength started to enter my mind.

There was also the slightest hope that our vague plans of escape would materialize. Weeks before departing we had contacted, through Polish workers, that underground organization of resistance and laid the groundwork for what we hoped would be a massive escape from the train. We had collected some jewelry and some valuables and sent them to the guerillas as payment. Somehow I didn't have much faith in this operation, but I know it brought a bit of hope to everyone. The whole thing had been organized with utmost secrecy. Only a few people—the leaders in our community—knew about it. It was planned that the underground would attack the train a few miles after leaving Pionki, in a very heavy forest area, so we could escape.

It never happened. Our train rumbled on through the forest without encountering any opposition. At the time, we felt betrayed. Years later we found out that the underground group actually did not betray us—they did attack a train and released all the people in it, but it was a different train, not ours.

***

We traveled for two or three days, and then arrived at the famous camp Theresienstadt. This camp was a model camp staged by the Nazis. Here, the International Red Cross had been invited to come and see for themselves how humanely Jews were being treated. Naturally, the Nazis claimed that all ghettos and camps were similar to Theresienstadt, and the entire world better take their word for it. In this "paradise" camp, indeed, life was decent. But it was only a facade. In the end, it was liquidated like all the other ones and everyone there ended up in Auschwitz.

We arrived tired, frightened, and cold, wrapped in blankets to try to protect us from the cold. Some young guys brought us hot food and toilet articles. We couldn't believe our luck. Our joy, however, was short lived. The camp authorities refused to receive our transport. They could not accommodate us. The camp was full. We were hustled back into the freight train.

We traveled in cramped and horrible conditions for a couple of days, making stops for food and for drink. At one of those stops we peered out the windows and saw people walking up and down alongside the train. We were still in Poland, this we knew. Someone suddenly knocked at our wagon and whispered, "Get out if you can. You are headed for Auschwitz, a concentration camp, and possible death."

It felt like the sky had come down on me and knocked me off balance.

It could not be.

Escape was impossible now. We spoke very little. For the first time I was overcome by a sense of impending doom. I was terrified. A few people started crying. Everyone was isolated with his or her own fears and thoughts.

Also, for the first time, I felt sorry for myself and angry at my father and sister and brother-in-law. It was because of them I was here now, facing the likely imminent end of my short, sweet life. My anger mounted. I hated them. I hated myself for being so soft hearted, for not making the right decision and staying in Pionki. Many other thoughts and strong emotions of remorse and regret entered my mind. Why, oh why, didn't I have enough guts? Why was I so naive as to believe in faith? Where the hell was the God that I had so recently felt close to?

We tried to survey the surroundings outside of our quietly passing train. We thought we were leaving Poland, forever. When I started writing this book, I thought that I had distinct memories of this train ride. I remembered the cold, the thirst, and the suffering of those around me. Recently though I have realized that my memories of this train ride are mixed and combined with other transfers, ones that were yet to happen to me in the future. Now, I do not feel comfortable ascribing specific details to this particular transfer by train. It was a terrible trip—and now it is blurred and buried in my mind.

When the train finally stopped it was in a visibly large, crowded camp. We were still in Poland. We had arrived at the world-famous Auschwitz, Birkenau section.

***

I could not end my story without accounting for what happened to me for the next many months until the end of the war. Mostly, this is a very sad story, and very difficult for me to relive.

Everyone is so horrified when they read about life in the camps. Everyone is moved to great pity. But, strangely enough, I have realized that experiencing it was more bearable than this—than reliving and redescribing it. When it was happening, I was in survival mode, like everyone else. When times were the worst, we didn't have time to think about anything except the next minute, the next hour, and how to survive to the next day. For a long time I could not bear to revisit my memories because of the sadness and depression that I felt, and the fear of stirring those sad feelings. I still feel the deep sadness—I always will. But my depression and despair have turned into a feeling of pride that I was able to survive at all. I am able to face my past without guilt or remorse, despite the tears.

For a long time, all I could endure remembering was up to the arrival at Auschwitz. I wrote in my journal, calling it "Remembrance," but then stopped when I got to that point.

What was it that prompted me to reopen that drawer and pull out those notes and memories in my journal? My daughter Susan's encouragement and prompting had a great effect. Also the general public's awakening interest in the Holocaust and the Jewish experience. There were suddenly many programs and television shows about it—shows like "Holocaust," "Winds of War," and "Playing for Time." I listened to people discuss and respond to these shows, and some asked me to verify the accuracy of the scenes they had seen portrayed. People started asking me about my own survival. I remember how astounded Joani, my younger daughter, was when she saw "Holocaust." She wanted to know more about my life during the war and was surprised at my secrecy about it. All of this influenced me to take up my pen again, and to see what could be done with the pile of notes in my journal. The TV programs, and reading Wouk's *War and Remembrance*, stirred so many memories that it was easy for me to begin again.

In 1985 I took a trip to Washington, DC for the American Gathering of Jewish Holocaust Survivors. The Gathering not only refreshed my memory of my frightful years in camps, but also of my life in Poland. It was to greet people I had known in my childhood, to reminisce about old times, to try to remember so many forgotten things, places, names. That made writing, which I love to do anyway, much easier. At the time I had been wondering why there was this awakening of interest in the Holocaust, after nearly forty years. Why now were people building memorials in Washington, Detroit, and other cities? It was at the gathering in DC that suddenly I got the answer. We survivors are elderly now, and many of us have adult children hungry for knowledge for our family histories.

That gathering was like coming to a huge family reunion and embracing hundreds of people one felt close to. All survivors have a lot in common. We all bear the deep emotional scars of losing our families and many dear ones in such a tragic way. How very gratifying it was for me to be there with my oldest daughter, Susan, and to give her a bit of insight into my past. After so many years of not discussing it, suddenly I could share. Suddenly my daughter was there, and I could lean on her and there was no fear of letting my painful memories come up. She could see and understand now the legacy that led to the phrase we repeated over and over again there. "Never again, never again."

Bolstered by my stirred emotions, by my determination that my family know their history, I begin where I left off years ago.

Auschwitz

We arrived in Auschwitz concentration camp. No orchestra, unlike in many movies made about Auschwitz, welcomed our transport.

The camp was enclosed by a barbed-wire fence. Dozens and dozens of barracks were lined up in a symmetrical order. It was an unbelievable sight of hordes of prisoners, all in striped uniforms. The whole area was surrounded by SS guards carrying clubs and whips. Tall chimneys dominated the huge area of the camp landscape. Those were the gas chambers. It was like entering a new planet. It all seemed so far-fetched and incredible. I suddenly remembered the encounter with the boy in Pionki who had told me about the deportation to the concentration camp Treblinka and the crematoriums there. Now, I finally believed him.

We arrived in Auschwitz and were housed in Camp B Birkenau, known to have been the largest detention center on earth. It housed more than one hundred thousand prisoners. We were "unloaded" and separated by sex. We were told later that we were so very lucky. Our transport from Pionki had mostly arrived safely and intact.

My father and I were pushed apart.

I looked at my frail father with such feelings of love and despair!

It was the very last time I would ever see him.

My Papa Tovy.

My devoted, loving Dad.

Quiet and often tired, devoted to the whole family.

I was told after the war that he struggled for several years longer and was killed in the concentration camp Mathausen in January 1945, only three months before liberation.

I stayed close to my sister Rella. Here, she saw her husband for the last time. He did not survive. We obeyed orders to strip and shower. We were too numb to think or worry about whether it would be water or gas that came down upon us. It was water.

After we showered we were given striped clothing. It was here that my shoes, those good shoes that my father made me, were taken away. What a mistake my father had made in making them so attractive and sturdy! Some other prisoners were allowed to keep their shoes, after having been stripped of all other belongings. But a female German guard noticed my good shoes and took them, giving me wooden ones instead. With those shoes went also my most valuable monetary possessions, the gold hidden in the heel.

We were then lined up to be tattooed on the left forearm. I still remember the number, which I had surgically removed long ago: A 15086.

The Nazis did all they could to dehumanize us. My tattoo transformed me into only a number, an object.

And then it was haircuts.

It was a Jewish girl doing the haircutting. She asked me if I had any hidden jewelry, in which case she would just trim and try to spare my hair. I was so shocked and hurt that I was about to have my hair cut off that I gave her a defiant stare. This infuriated her. She promptly shaved my head.

There I was—shaved, in striped clothing, wooden shoes, and, despite the fact that I should have considered myself lucky to still be living at all, the humiliation and degradation I felt at that moment is hard to describe. Such doom came over me, such despair and complete resignation, that without hesitation I broke free of the group and ran toward the huge fence around the compound, which I knew would electrocute me within a few feet of it. My sister saw me and started screaming. Someone ran after me and brought me back.

So began our life in Auschwitz.

Transports arrived almost daily. Some people were dead on arrival because of the heat and lack of water. At times you could see smoke from the chimneys. We had heard about the crematoriums, which Jews had been forced to construct. I heard from the other girls that thousands of human beings we were told were crammed into them and asphyxiated all at once and then disposed of under the watchful eyes of the SS. The goal was the quickest destruction of all the Jews in the most secretive manner. This was Hitler's "final solution"—the extermination of all Europe's Jews to make the world "pure."

If you read recent books about the Holocaust, most

of them refer to the date of the decision to totally exterminate the Jews as of January, 1942. The Wannsee Conference was where the "final solution" and how to achieve it was decided. It seems unreal to me that the Nazis were able to conceal for years the true extent of their brutal atrocities. It is amazing that they got away with it. I guess they had guts and ingenuity. It also still continues to puzzle me how citizens of a basically very civilized country so overwhelmingly followed Hitler, this pathological monster, although much has been written in an effort to discuss and explain this phenomenon. Why did the Nazis blame the Jews for all their political and economic problems?

I often wondered why, if the allies were aware of the existence of the gas chambers, did they not bomb them? It would have been so easy. We watched the planes flying over us so low! We stood outside in our striped clothing and waved to them. Tens of thousands of lives could have been spared!

There was a discussion about this recently during a TV interview with Sir Martin Gilbert. The simple answer that is most often heard is that they needed the bombs in order to destroy railroads and factories, to help the war efforts. But there was another reason that has been proposed too. Some think that the US government did not want it to be looked upon as a "Jewish War." They did not want to stir up anti-Semitism in this country. Even the Jewish members of our government agreed with this tactic.

So no one was eager to activate any rescue attempts, and no one took any measures even to halt the program of genocide.

***

During one of the grueling roll calls (they forever counted us!), I recall an incident that clearly reflects my state of mind while I was in Auschwitz.

As I wrote earlier, I had a dear high school friend, David Eiger, whose father was my father's CPA and also a good friend of my parents. Mr. Eiger, as it turned out, had endured Auschwitz for a year or longer and had achieved an administrative position, or what was called the status of an "Elder."

Standing at a roll call, I saw Mr. Eiger walking by me with a group of SS men. I lowered my head in shame, hoping he would not recognize me.

Obviously, I should have done the opposite, and taken pains that he did recognize me. To know someone with authority could have made an important difference in my fate. But my sense of despair and shame at my wretched appearance was too great. At the time, I had rather he didn't see me.

But Mr. Eiger did recognize me and when he passed he whispered, "Your dad is okay. I just saw him. Keep your spirits up. I'll try to keep in touch." I was bewildered and numb. I don't remember how I answered, or if I did at all.

I never saw Mr. Eiger after that encounter. I know that he did survive the war, but died a few years later. I did keep in touch with his son David who also survived and who eventually moved to the US and lived in Minneapolis. I saw his sister Dora in Washington during the Gathering of Survivors—a great reunion!

***

I was lucky. I stayed in Auschwitz only five days.

On my fifth day at Auschwitz, SS held a nude inspection. We paraded in front of several SS officers. Anyone with a blemish was set aside, never to return.

I held on to my sister, but she was told to join the line to the right. I followed her—this was not allowed—they sent me to the left. We were separated, and I did not see her until seven months after the war ended.

I looked, I guess, healthy enough and was chosen with a group of others to be sent to work at an ammunition factory in Hindenburg.

Hindenburg

The town of Hindenburg was located in the southeast corner of Germany near the Polish border. We were assigned to work in a factory manufacturing, to the best of my knowledge, airplane or tank parts. The factory operated under the auspices of Auschwitz. It was a humane and decent place.

Obviously I was happy to get out of Auschwitz, but I felt so lost, so alone, without my sister Rella. I was so worried about her being left behind! So suddenly I had lost the only family I had left, and the only dear and close human being whom I had finally learned to love, appreciate, and depend on. None of my friends were in this group of eighty to one hundred girls either. I missed my dearest friend Andzia. I missed her deep concern and her devotion to me.

Nothing is as terrifying as the unknown. In Hindenburg I was uprooted, terrified of tomorrow, and of all the tomorrows that I would have to face alone.

***

We were housed in barracks divided into large sections of about twenty girls per room. The rooms were immaculate. Floors and furniture were scrubbed daily, we showered every morning, and our striped clothing was literally boiled every single day. Why all this cleanliness and precaution? We came in contact with the Germans in the factory and they worried about filth and disease.

We slept in double bunk beds on mattresses filled with straw. I remember that I slept in the upper bunk. Every morning I meticulously smoothed the bulky mattress and carefully formed it to a perfect and precise shape, covered with a blanket. I was repeatedly praised for this attention to detail. To this day I am a little bit of a fanatic about the neatness of my bed.

I volunteered for the night shift in the welding department. I remember picking up the work without much difficulty. I learned quickly how to weld two parts of something or other together. Now, whenever I see a welder on television or in life, with his masks and gloves and sparks flying from the unit he is working on, my thoughts go back to my days as a welder. The supervisors at work treated us coldly but humanely.

Before I had a chance to perfect my skill as a welder I was transferred to a much better job. Although I was reasonably healthy, I was not prepared for, nor could easily endure, the twelve-hour-day factory work. There were many girls in our group who were much more accustomed to hard work. They felt sorry for me and tried to help me at all times, so when the supervisor asked for someone who knew German and would be capable of handling inventory control of the parts and tools department, my name was quickly suggested.

I held this job for a few weeks, did well, and was promoted to a more prestigious job soon after. This was a wonderful break for me, and how grateful I was for my knowledge of the German language.

We in Hindenburg were in a completely separate camp, but because we were under the auspices of Auschwitz we had to endure monthly SS visits, countless inspections, medical check-ups, and even a monthly visit from a dentist who pulled on the spot any tooth with a minor cavity. Our direct factory employers and supervisors, however, were members of the Wehrmacht—army draftees—not SS or Gestapo. They were scared German citizens and even though they tried to follow orders from the Nazis, they still treated us humanely, even kindly at times.

We got used to the regimentation. After the morning showers and breakfast of a piece of bread, we marched in the middle of the road about one mile to work. We were a pathetic-looking group—a few dozen undernourished girls in striped clothes—marching to work guarded by armed soldiers.

I remember many instances when during our marches to or from work I saw German women's eyes filled with tears. Perhaps they were crying because the sight of us reminded them to be worried about their own husbands and sons on the front. Some of the women tried throwing us parcels of bread and toilet articles. They did this even though the guards would chase them away.

The war conditions were obviously deteriorating

for the Germans. More and more older men were being drafted, some reservists were reclassified for active duty, and all were petrified of being shipped to the Russian front. We girls that could understand German picked up this information from conversations that we overheard. The factory was shorthanded. Women took over many management positions and help was desperately needed for simple office duties.

Relatively speaking, I was very lucky and my new job was fantastic. With my promotion, I was the new assistant to the purchasing agent. It was forbidden for a Jew to hold such a position. During inspections, my supervisors used to hide me in a closet. My knowledge of German must have been flawless and without an accent because I even handled the phone at times. My typing must have improved too.

My boss was a middle-aged man (he must have been in his late '40s, which seemed old at the time). He was a quiet man and scared to even converse with me beyond the duties of my job. But he was a kind person, and showed me kindness in many ways. He corrected my work, never complained, and he sometimes would leave part of his lunch, knowing well that after he left his office I would eat it. He was afraid to give it to me openly, so he would at times order an extra soup or tell me to "dispose" of the leftovers, which he would have wrapped back up carefully and placed in the wastepaper basket, and then he would leave the office for a while.

Gratefully I would eat whatever he left, or would save it to share later with my friends. His leftovers were a lifesaver!

It seems too funny to describe, this crazy fear that the Germans had of the Nazis. They were so concerned to obey orders, even when they seemed disturbed by the cruelty they were participating in. I guess this explains how Hitler was able to control the masses.

I am sure I was envied for this easy job in a warm office when many of the people worked outside in the bitter cold. I was envied, but I don't think that I was resented. My privilege embarrassed me and I tried to make up for it in many ways. One of my duties as purchasing assistant was to check the incoming inventory materials which usually arrived by rail. It was my friends who unloaded it. I often tried to help with unloading, but was usually shoved aside by the guards. Very often my boss was out of the office and when this happened I would sneak in a few girls at a time to the office to warm up. I shared the bit of extra food and always offered a word of hope.

I was the camp's leading optimist. Every evening the girls gathered around me hungry for reassurance, for a lift of their spirits, for a boost of morale. I kept my own doubts and fears to myself because I knew how much the others depended on me. How I missed my dear sister! How often I thought about her.

We looked over the fence of our encampment sometimes and watched the normal life taking place out there. We tried to joke about the women wearing silk stockings and dresses or suits and hats, and compared their outfits to ours which we were handed each morning—oddly colored socks, head scarves that did not at all match our striped clothing, and gloves with holes in them. We knew also that our faces were gaunt, drab, shabby. Our food consisted of mostly stale bread, coffee, and soup. (Truthfully I don't think the Germans ate much better by the end of the war.) I used to crave for a fresh roll and fresh fruit. We used to talk about it and joke about it and dream about it.

I think a purposeful effort towards optimism is contagious. It certainly added to my own strength, determination, and will to live. Except for a few dark moments, this attitude prevailed in me throughout all the war years, to the very end.

I was always so terribly hungry. These kinds of circumstances drove many people to resort to selfishness, in their fight to survive day by day. There were many times when the piece of bread I had saved to eat later was stolen from under my pad.

The "Elders" in all the camps were the Jews among us, either voted in or volunteers. They mostly tried to please the Germans—some were outright cruel in the hopes that this would save their skins or garner them more privileges. Others, however, worked hard to reduce hardships. Some, in several camps, saved many Jewish lives. After the war some of those Jews who had held prestigious or management positions in the camps, under the supervision of the Gestapo, had fears of reprisal because of their cruel treatment of fellow Jews. Some settled in remote areas, scared to face the other survivors. I myself cannot truly condemn them. We all tried, in one way or another, to survive.

The months were passing. We had hopes that we might wait out the war in our currently pretty secure surroundings at Hindenburg. Life, after all, was bearable here. The drab days were passing quickly. I think that I enjoyed the cleanliness the most. The immaculate order helped to make up for the hunger and despair at times.

We heard many rumors. Rumors about Hitler's attempted assassination, about the state of the war, we even heard about the Normandy invasion and the American involvement in the war. Now we embraced new hope! We saw the deterioration of the German spirit. We knew they were fighting a losing war, but how long, how long?

These rumors spread among us when we overheard bits of news on the radio, or from what we were told by the Polish prisoners of war who worked nearby at the railroad. We had opportunities for fairly frequent interaction with these Polish prisoners because our factory received shipments by rail, and during unloading we would be close enough to exchange words with the Poles. We girls were not allowed to have any contact with outsiders, so all our communication had to be done in utmost secrecy and with great caution in order to evade the watchful eye of the guards. And at times the Poles threw little parcels of food, soap, toothpaste, and such over the tracks.

Because of my special job, I was able to move around more freely, and was not watched as closely as the others. I had more liberty to be a little closer to the Polish prisoners of war. One of the men even became an admirer—he took a fancy to me, and one time even suggested that we meet after the war. I exchanged several notes with this man. Mine were written usually in utmost secrecy, usually in total darkness under a blanket. I had to hide this kind of activity from everyone because, honestly, you could never be sure who could be trusted and who would betray you. I always wore my red gloves so that "my" Polish prisoner connection could identify me from all the other girls in striped clothes, from a distance. One time I remember standing near the German guard and my Polish friend dared to walk over to me, within two or three feet. I felt so ashamed suddenly of my shorn head. I wasn't wearing a head scarf and my hair was still very, very short. Even after all the degradation, I still had female pride and self-consciousness!

A few of us were caught one time when we were sneaking in some food and toiletries (smuggled to us by the Polish prisoners of war) to camp. Naturally we did not betray the source, so shortly thereafter the four or five of us that were involved were called into the commander's office to be interrogated.

For the first time in months I was very scared. I was petrified, and shaking so badly that I feared my knees would give way. The commander was a rather rough, cruel man, and we were all going to be interrogated separately.

When he opened the door the first time and called for the first girl to enter, I walked in. My intuition told me that perhaps he would not be as enraged at the beginning of the process as he would be later. I think that I was right. I told him that we found the stuff by the railroad. He kicked me and slapped me, and then shoved me out the door.

The last girl suffered the worst beating. She was a beautiful, talented young singer from Vienna. She had always been our nightingale and brought many times a sparkle of culture and joy to us through her music. I think that she had been a daughter of a cantor, for she sang at times cantorial songs and once chanted the Yom Kippur liturgy sung on Kol Nidre night. Needless to say, it was impossible to describe our emotions that night. For all my life since the war, cantorial music will deeply move me, and often brings me to tears.

A very memorable incident was our first Christmas in Hindenburg. The camp commander asked us to put on a show and entertain his soldiers for Christmas. A group of us, including the singer from Vienna, wrote and staged a show. How vividly I remember making costumes from scarves and socks for the performance! With no supplies, only a bit of imagination, we put together the Christmas show. We even made, I remember, scenery!

All the soldiers and guards gathered to see the performance. They were in general passive people, just doing their jobs, not particularly mean and not especially thoughtful. They seemed wooden most of the time because, I presume, to carry out orders they had to suppress their feelings.

But that night was different.

Our show was a success and to end it my friend from Vienna sang "My Yiddishe Mama" in German. This was very daring of her.

I saw many tears running down the tough German faces. The next day many of them openly brought us their ration of bread and whatever else they could spare.

That beautiful and talented girl from Vienna started

ailing soon after and died before we left Hindenburg, perhaps from the beating she had received from the commander.

***

The sirens blared more often now. The Allies' bombing was much more frequent. The Germans ran to the bunkers. We didn't bother. We waved to the Allied planes instead.

I held on to my red wool gloves, my identity tag for my Polish connection. One morning my Polish friend waved and motioned that he was going to pass me an important note, and that I should get nearer to the guard. I moved over to where he had indicated, and he did the same. The guard objected to us being so close, but my friend told him he wanted to see my warm red gloves. I handed my glove to the guard and he handed it to the Pole. My friend pretended to examine it, and exclaimed over it, and I saw him slipping a note into it. When I put my glove back on I felt the paper. Our procedure had worked—so idiotic what we had to go through!—but I felt my heart pounding because we could have been so severely punished.

That night some girls—the few other ones that I trusted—and I read that important note. We read it in a remote area, and then destroyed it. The contents were startling indeed. The note said, "The Russian troops are on the move and will be in this area in three or four days. My advice to you is: Gather some food and hide in the camp or surrounding forest area. I suspect that you will be shipped out immediately."

The news of his plan created a turmoil in my mind. Should I trust him? If the end of the war is so near, perhaps the Germans would leave us. Should we wait to be liberated? Or should I take his advice and hide? I thought about my options and suggested to a friend that perhaps we should hide in one of the huge soup kettles (many were empty in a warehouse). But upon further consideration, decided that I was too scared. All my life I had believed in *bashert*, God's will, and I also believed that God's will would favor me since, after all, I had been born in a caul, remember? I decided to stay and hope that the Germans, panicking with the end of the war, would just leave us and run.

And so we stayed.

Tremendous tumult and confusion took over in the factory. My boss left suddenly. I was told that he was drafted into active service. I was left alone in the department, scared, and answering calls from high government officials. Everyone was in an uproar. It was clear that Germany was beginning to crumble. We saw signs and preparation for retreat. We felt that the storm was almost over. We would witness the end and the end for us was so near!

We waited.

But how right he was, my Polish friend! Suddenly, shortly after he had tried to warn me, we were all hastily loaded into a freight train, and our journey to the next dreadful location started.

Bergen Belsen

We traveled through a most beautiful mountainous countryside. The snow whitened the countryside, and the mountains seen from the distance were so very beautiful, so serene! I promised myself to return, if I lived to be free again, to see this area from near, to touch, to taste again the beautiful clean snow.

We traveled for at least three days. I can't remember being hungry—though I am sure we were—but I know we must have been thirsty because we engineered a way of getting some clean snow through the high and barred little window. We attached a rope to a can and pulled the lowered can along the ground, outside of the moving train. It collected snow and we lifted it through the little window. The snow tasted good, but it left us thirstier yet.

I remember all the resigned, frightened faces, the helplessness and fear. I turned to silent prayer, the first time in a long time, and asked God for strength as I plunged again into the unknown.

The train stopped; we all got out. We had arrived in the world-famous, notorious, worst of all concentration camps—the death camp of Bergen Belsen, housing about one hundred thousand women. There were no gas chambers, they didn't need them. Many thousands did not survive even weeks there. It was a nightmare camp. Over the course of the war, seventy thousand women perished there.

I don't think that I'll go into detail of my misery there. I don't think it's necessary. But I can't skip over it completely.

I have wanted to tell it for so many years! How easy I find doing it now. I am surprised that thoughts come to mind and it is not difficult to put it on paper. It's funny how, writing this, I feel like that was another me I am writing about.

How could I have endured it?

How could I have had the will, the guts, to even continue to live?

***

There were about nine hundred girls in the one barracks I was housed in. There were dozens and dozens of other barracks exactly like it in Bergen Belsen. We slept on pads on the floor, suffering starvation, with nothing to do.

There were no showers, no toilet facilities, barely any food. We were filthy, smelly, diseased, covered with lice, and starving. People were dying all around us and sometimes it took a while before they were pulled out of the barracks. So we just stepped over the dead bodies to go outside. The smell was unbelievable.

And—they counted us and counted us every day. I barely had the strength to stand. I was starving. It's hard to describe how it feels to be so hungry. There is such a feeling of desperation. It overwhelms you. You no longer care.

The optimism and faith that had kept me going for so long now dimmed to a shadow. Such sadness and despair overcame me! I wondered often what wrong had I done in life, why was I being punished? Why me? I had always thought that I was a good person. So, why, why me? I remember, I found a mirror once, or a resemblance of a mirror, and I looked at my sad, hopeless face and I wondered what I would look like smiling. It was impossible for me to even form a smile.

I know now what the word "depression" really means.

There were so many sleepless nights. I would lie awake and listen to the deadly quiet, not hearing even a bird outside. Those nights, my thoughts would wander back to my childhood—to all those happy and carefree years, to my dear family. I prayed for strength, but at times I hated God. I felt betrayed.

And yet, somehow, as always before with me, this enormous will to live remained, and perhaps made my survival possible.

At some point I got sick with typhoid fever. I still had to stand daily for roll call. Those endless roll calls. Why did they forever have to count us? I never disclosed to authorities my illness because I would have been taken to the "hospital" from which no one ever returned.

My instinct directed me in ways to survive. I saw girls dying like flies from disease and from dysentery. I suspected the drinking water was either polluted or poisoned. So, even when I was at my sickest, I carried pails of water to my pad and dunked my head and arms to reduce the fever. I did not drink the water. I might have lost my optimism, but not my fighting spirit. I was not going to be as resigned as most. Human bodies can endure more than anyone can imagine.

We were rotting on a cold floor in our barracks in filth, smells, disease . . . and we could not believe how little the world cared. We could not believe how long this war lasted and that no rescue was even attempted. We could not understand how long Germany could hold out.

I knew the end was very near and I knew that I had to fight to survive.

There were some fortunate girls who had jobs working in the kitchen. Helen Adler was one of them. She was my sister's friend, and she saw me one day during my illness. She brought me some sugar. Every day thereafter she brought some soup and little bits of sugar—a teaspoon or less, which she stole. I think it saved my life. How glad I was many years later to repay her kindness! (I cared for her when she was sick during her trip to the United States from Israel.)

Very few girls were so thoughtful. People became like animals, stealing bread from one another, and anything else that they could.

I started slowly to recover. I was frail and weak, but I was also defiant and knew that I would keep up the fight to survive. I got a job carrying soup kettles to the barracks, and for this work I got an extra soup. I remember sharing it at times with the less fortunate and frail girls who were in the barracks near me. How gratifying it was to receive, years later, a letter from someone in Australia in which she recalled my concern and kindness. She visited me years later in the US, she and her husband spent several days in my home, but I did not even remember her face or her name, and to this day I cannot remember which starving shadow of a girl was my roommate on the floor of Bergen Belsen.

Those kettles were very heavy—I was still weak and could barely carry them—so I decided to try to get a kitchen job. I stood in line for days and did finally get a job in the kitchen peeling potatoes. I could eat all the peel of the raw potatoes I wanted. It was food! The kitchen job was a Godsend. But I must have worked there no more than a week or so when I noticed a small irritation on my hand. I disregarded it at the time, but it eventually developed into an infection that almost cost me my right arm and my life. I began to feel hot and feverish.

I did not know that liberation was only days off. I stopped thinking ahead.

I was so ill. I figured it must be spring already, it must be Passover time. We were mute most of the time, nothing to talk about and no strength to do so. So I talked silently with God and made another deal. I promised Him that if I recovered and survived, Passover holidays would always be special and I would make an effort for it to be festive and sharing. I did keep my promise and I always think about it at every year at Passover time.

I was always making deals with God and had many, many weeks and months in which to contemplate and pray and cry, until tears no longer came.

I was usually up at dawn. There were only three wash-basins and three water faucets outside for all eight hundred or nine hundred women in our barracks. Being up so early I was able to use it before everybody, under the watchful eyes of the guard, outside in the high tower. I would crawl between the sleeping live and dead bodies, and I would get to those water faucets. I did not drink, but I did wash off. It cooled me. But the fever continued and I was shaking and scared.

Liberation ~
April 15, 1945

On the morning of April 15, 1945, I was up very early, as usual, to get to the water faucets outside. I looked up, and could see the watch tower empty. Puzzled, I ventured a few steps further and noticed the next tower empty also. The surroundings were very still, no one in sight. I saw the first daylight of the morning. Scared but bewildered I walked further and then suddenly, amazed, I saw a white flag on a distant building—and there were no Germans in sight.

I ran back to my barracks screaming, "We are free! We are free! The Germans are gone!"

It would take a much more talented writer than me to describe the scenes that followed.

Hundreds, and then thousands, of skeleton-like figures came running to the front gates, screaming hysterically. I was up near the very front, and was pressed up against the wire fence, and could see the first British tank as it came rolling into camp.

Many more followed it. Through the loudspeaker, with tear-filled voices, they repeated over and over again in several languages, "You are free. We are with the British Army. Be calm, be calm. Food and help is on the way."

In June of 2005 my daughter Debbie was watching the PBS program *Frontline: Remembering the Camps*, in which they showed footage from the liberation of Bergen Belsen. My daughter was startled to see me, up against the fence, in the first minutes of the film waving to the first British tanks entering the camp. I wrote to PBS and they sent me a video copy of the film, and the somewhat blurry picture of me cut from it. I asked PBS for permission to include this photo in my book and was referred to the original owners of that film, the Imperial War Museum in London. It was Mr. Roger Smither, Keeper of the Film and Photograph Archives Department, who dug into his records and had the museum

Day of Liberation. I am waving to the first British troops entering Bergen Belsen. April 15, 1945. I am in the front row, center.

photo department make a clearer "frame grab" blow up (a still photograph from the original footage of the film taken more than sixty years ago.)

The film is preserved in the film and video archives of the Imperial War Museum in London, UK. Mr. Smither also mailed me a copy of the "dope sheet" (the Army Film Unit cameraman's written description that accompanied the film). Mr. Smither knew the cameraman, Sgt. Mike Lewis, who happened to be Jewish.

Here is an excerpt of British Sergeant Mike Lewis's written report of the film he took while entering Bergen Belsen:

With the advance of the British troops into Germany, confirmation comes to light of the brutalities and horror unequaled in the memory of man. Such a confirmation is the camp near Belsen. As far as I can see they are divided up into camps for men, women, political, criminal (although what is criminal in German eyes is hard to imagine), and Typhus cases. In all it is estimated at sixty thousand people. In those camps are people from all of Europe. There are German and Hungarian guards left in camp and acting under our orders. Each individual British soldier is looked upon as those people's deliverer from hell upon earth.

The PBS *Frontline* documentary film told an interesting story of how the British Army discovered the Bergen Belsen camp. The army was in Northern Germany in mid-April of 1945. They stopped near the town of Bergen Belsen. They admired the pretty country-side, the calm surroundings, but they were puzzled by a strange and awful smell that didn't seem to fit in the clean farming community. They followed this smell and discovered the unbelievable existence of the Bergen Belsen death camps.

* * *

Amidst all the chaos, somehow the British army set up stands with food and medical tents. I think that the soldiers who first entered our camp were so shocked and so horrified that it took much longer to organize in this terrible chaos than I remember. The soldiers opened the nearby men's camp, which we hadn't even known existed.

How can I describe the scene of fathers finding daughters, wives finding husbands, sisters finding brothers? How can I describe those unbelievable hours?

I, however, found no one. No family, not even any friends.

My infected arm was badly swollen and there was a dark red strip running up the inside. I knew that I had a temperature. I made my way to the medical aid tents. An English army doctor made an incision and left the wound open for the puss to drain. There was a lot of it. I remember it splattered on the doctor's coat. The swelling continued upwards over my elbows. I ran a high temperature. I knew this was a very bad sign, and I was frantic. I didn't want to die now! Not after all we'd been through. I was free now! I had *seen* my own liberation!

The cleanup and body burning began. The British Army moved us to new barracks that had previously been occupied by the German Army and then proceeded to burn the entire disease-infested camps of Bergen Belsen. There were many piles of dead bodies that went up in smoke.

I went to see the English doctor again the next day. The swelling had worsened. His decision was to amputate my right arm the next day. He said it was necessary in order to save my life. I came back to the new barracks and cried as never before. I decided not to return to the first aid tent. I felt that I would rather die than live as a cripple. That night, after I had cried myself to sleep, I had a dream that I will never forget. I saw my mother. She took me in her arms and assured me that my arm would heal, and would be as good as new, normal and strong, and told me not to hesitate, and to go back to the tent.

The next morning, I went back to the first aid tent.

There was a nurse working there who knew me—she was from my hometown—and she begged the doctor to help me. She told him that I was her relative. With much reluctance, he authorized to give me a shot of penicillin—the last and only one he had.

That one shot of penicillin did wonders, but to this day, I believe that it was my wonderful Mom that watched over me from heaven above and saved my arm and my life. I don't see my mother in my dreams often, but over the years, whenever I do, bad news follows. It never fails. Is she warning me and at the same time watching over me?

I probably needed more than that one dose of penicillin, because I continued to be ill for several months afterward. I was sent to a makeshift hospital and they cut my arm open again for drainage. I continued to run a high temperature. There were so many ill people that I received no care at all at that hospital. They washed me once in two or three days, handed me soup and bread, and let me just lie there. I was worried that I would just die and rot there.

My determination and intense will to live prevailed again. One day I pulled myself out of bed and got dressed and just walked out of the hospital to a nearby dorm where I knew some survivors were housed. That was as far as I could make it. I collapsed at their doorstep. They took me in, cared for me, and nursed me back to health.

***

It is very difficult to describe the weeks that followed. Thousands and thousands of newly freed survivors started traveling from one camp to another throughout Germany, France, and Poland, looking for family, friends, and for any familiar faces. I could not travel yet, after the illness, but I put my name on every available list. The Red Cross did a superb job of putting people in touch with one another that way.

So many happy, anxious faces! So many tears!

There were lists and lists of survivors posted at all train depots. I, like thousands of others, went to the station every day to read those lists. I checked names with eager hope and anticipation. I checked and checked, but found no family, no friends, no familiar names among the lists of survivors.

The *blitzkrieg*, the war that was supposed to be lightning-quick, had lasted almost five long years. I was all alone, in this strange, hateful country of Germany, with nowhere to go and no one to share my miraculous survival. I could not, because of my illness, return to Poland to the Kubicka family as my parents had arranged for us to do in case of separation, so long ago. People had been arriving in our camp from Poland too, but there was no one I knew. It felt pointless to return there now.

One day in the Deplaced Persons camp, at last, I was visited by someone dear to me. And it was none other my old boyfriend, Moniek Horowich. A girl who knew me from before the war had wanted to surprise him, and brought him to me. She was hoping to witness the surprise embrace of old friends.

He looked and looked at me, and I will never forget the first words he uttered, they startled me so much.

"You look familiar," he said.

I know I looked like a shadow then, and probably weighed no more than eighty pounds.

After the first shock of how much I had changed, Moniek cared for me with a fatherly love and affection. He stayed on in camp and did all that he could for me. He brought me additional food, like fresh milk and eggs from the farm, and extra clothing. He looked and felt surprisingly good.

Weeks later he found out that his mother and wife had survived. He had married during the war. He left the camp to go and join them.

I started gaining weight and strength and my arm partially healed. I was so anxious to return to more normal living conditions, so tired of standing in line for food, so tired of the group life.

It was then that two boys I knew from Radom stopped in our camp and told us of an enchanting little town they had passed through, one of the very few not touched by bombing. It was a town called Bad Nauheim, settled in the mountains near Frankfort on Main, an area occupied currently by the Americans. They urged us to go there. All of us survivors received free passes for travel by train anywhere. The offer and the prospect were tempting. Later I found out that President Roosevelt frequented Bad Nauheim before the war because it was a well-known health resort. That is possibly why it was spared the devastating bombing that reduced so much of the rest of Germany to rubble.

I was told that I needed more care and more nourishing food in order for my arm to heal completely. With tens of thousands of survivors to care for, our British liberators simply didn't have the medical facilities or proper goods to rectify all the damage the Nazis had done to so many human beings. We were told that the Americans had an abundance of food, facilities, and medicine.

I talked one of the other girls into venturing with me on a trip to this promising little town of Bad Nauheim. I knew I needed a change of scene. I didn't know that I would find there a new life, the love of my life, and a budding future.

Bad Nauheim~
September 1945

Bad Nauheim was truly a dream. Untouched by bombings, nestled in the mountains, it looked its part as a well-known health resort. My friend and I arrived there by train at the beginning of September 1945, about five months after we were liberated. Several more fami-

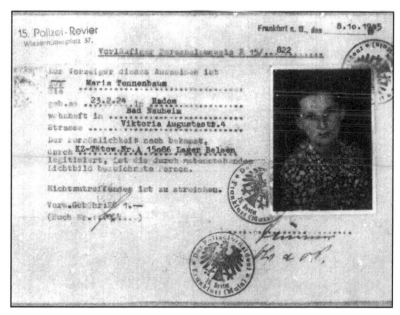

This is my first German-police-issued document in Bad Nauheim. Note the identification number 15086—it's the number that was tattooed on my arm by the Nazis.

lies came soon afterwards to this quaint and charming little town, among them the two boys who had initially told us about it.

We rented a room from a German family. The lady of the house was cordial, but not very communicative. We obtained from local authorities a Displaced Persons card, which entitled us to a little money, ration cards, and free travel. Our room was on the third floor of the building. For the first time in years I slept in a normal bed with white linens. I cried with joy the first night. What luxury! How indescribably wonderful it felt.

We found our way to the American Army headquarters and we both got jobs with the American unit located in town, setting tables. We wanted this job because we hoped that it would give us access to extra food. Indeed, when we were hired, they took us to the kitchen and the cook was told to give us any food we liked. They told us to eat as much as we wanted to. The Americans had an abundance of fresh wholesome food. No one would believe me but the first few days I ate an incredible amount of food (eight eggs for breakfast!).

I saw a local German specialist who checked and X-rayed my arm and assured me that, although badly scarred, my arm would be normal and that there was no bone damage. I thought of the dream I had about my mother predicting it, and cried.

It was so peaceful and beautiful to feel semi-normal again, and so wonderful to be free to talk without a shadow of the German guard behind me, and to be able to smile again! But also I felt so sad to have lost all my

Marty in Germany.

Marty at his desk in Germany.

loved ones. I made no plans for the future. I concentrated on living in and trying to enjoy the present fully.

Downstairs in the building where we were living now was the office of the American Military Police, the "MP."

One day my friend and I saw a Jewish survivor being escorted by the MP to the office downstairs. Sensing a problem we waited outside. It turned out to be a minor misunderstanding (he wore an army cap and was questioned about it). More importantly, the interpreter in the MP office was no other than Martin Salinger. He was a prosecutor for the MPs. He was startled to hear, from the survivor that had been brought to him, that there were other Jewish survivors in this town (my friend and I were among the very first of many who would arrive.) Marty escorted the boy outside, wishing to speak with him further. The boy pointed to us standing nearby, indicating that we were part of the Jewish group in town. That was the way I met Martin Salinger, who was soon to become my husband. Years later the boy was proud to claim to have been the matchmaker.

Marty, being as sensitive and caring then as he was throughout our marriage, simply offered his help to the community of survivors, and could not do enough for us. He immediately took a liking to the two of us girls who were his upstairs neighbors. He seemed especially interested in me, but romance was quite far from my mind and I used to talk my friend into keeping him company.

Marty brought us not only cheer but also food, cigarettes, and anything extra that he could. I found him very pleasant and warm, but did not even allow myself to think any further.

I had other things on my mind.

I was worried that I had still not regained my period yet, which had stopped during the war. The other girls I knew were already back to normal. I worried a bit about my arm, which was still healing, but with slow progress.

I had also received several warm and inviting letters from friends who had survived and were settled now in Stuttgart, Germany. Chaim Mandelbaum, Leon Bergeisen, Andzia and several others—all very close, old, and dear friends. They were now together in a Displaced Person's camp, and urged me to come join them. I was very tempted and considered leaving Bad Nauheim shortly to join them. Marty, however, was very persistent in his continued interest in me. He pleaded for me to stay a little longer.

I will never forget our walk in the beautiful park when he first kissed me. All my resistance melted away.

After that moment, we spent every possible minute together.

Those were the days of tenderness and gentle love and such peace. We spent many long hours going for walks hand in hand or just sitting on a park bench watching children playing and watching the trees changing beautiful colors. We were in a cloud.

It was like a beautiful dream, after the tragedy and turmoil of the preceding years.

After having known me for only two weeks, Marty asked me to marry him. His words were "I fell in love with you the moment I saw you. I want to marry you and take you to the United States." I laughed at first—I barely knew him! I felt so secure with him, so totally happy, but it had all happened so quickly! I wanted to get to know him better. But Marty was very worried that

On this bridge Marty proposed marriage to me.

he would be transferred and then might lose me. He wanted to start working on all the complicated paperwork. Also, the American army law was firm in forcing a ninety day "cooling off" period for any GI marrying a foreigner.

He took me in his arms and I knew I'd never find anyone else. We were together constantly. It seemed so secure and peaceful after all the nightmares.

There was a Mr. Fried in Bad Nauheim who knew my father and he absolutely forbid me to marry Marty. He was worried that Marty might have a wife and kids in the United States. I laughed at the idea. I was totally happy and trusting.

As the reality of my new situation set in, however, there were some fears that sometimes felt overwhelming. "This young American is from a strange land," I thought. "His family will surely resent me. I don't know their language, their way of life. How could I suddenly trust my life with this man and his new world?" The only language we both knew and conversed in was German. The only other thing that we had in common was our religion. I feared my arrival in Detroit. I feared his family's acceptance of me and even suggested that we move to another city, even another country! Marty wrote to his family about the Jewish girl from Poland that he intended to marry. He received an anxious letter from his older brother Joe trying to discourage him, promising him financial help upon return to the States and warning him of the "dangers" of such a marriage. Polish Jews were considered socially beneath Lithuanian Jews—which Marty was. I didn't even know Hebrew or Yiddish language, and when I wrote a letter to my potential new family they replied, "What kind of Jew is it writing us a letter in Polish?" This was discouraging for me. "Could love overcome so many real-life obstacles, and the fears those obstacles stirred?" I wondered.

But Marty was so reassuring and so loving and he nullified my worries and anxieties. There could have been many foreseeable problems in our future, but when I was with him, this young corporal I found myself so in love with, I became blind and deaf to all those problems.

He set the wedding date to be December 11—exactly ninety days from the day that we filled out the permit papers. We wired to his family announcing the day, and after that we received congratulatory letters and several parcels.

One time Marty had asked me to go for a walk to a nearby park. It was fall, cool outside, and I did not own a sweater or a jacket. I had been too embarrassed to say so and my roommate had offered me hers to borrow. Marty had understood, and wired his sister in Detroit to send sweaters, jackets, and "anything you can." When those parcels arrived, what a joy it was to receive a dress, sweaters, and other nice accessories!

In one parcel they had also included a box of pancake mix. I will never forget how Marty tried to explain this new and strange food to me, and how I tried to make something of it, but my attempts yielded nothing edible and finally I just threw it out. There was so much to learn, so many strange and new things to comprehend!

Marty and me outside the synagogue two months before our wedding. This was possibly the only remaining synagogue in Germany after the war.

***

The population of survivors living in Bad Nauheim now had grown to about forty people. We all lived in a building that we took over on Carlstrasse. It was a *pensione*, a senior retirement home before. We were like a big, happy family living in comfort and with joy. Many were still trav-

Marty and me attending services; we are in the balcony, third and fourth from the right.

eling through the country, searching for and visiting others who had survived.

One day when I was at our apartment a friend of mine dropped in for a surprise visit. She brought with her another girl. I embraced my friend, and then turned to meet the new girl. It took several seconds before I recognized who the other visitor was—and with what joy and what shock—it was my sister Rella!

It had been seven months since liberation. What a reunion!

What happiness that moment brought me! Rella had just arrived from Radom. She had been liberated by the Russians, and then returned to Radom. After she had heard recently that I too was still alive, she had traveled nonstop for several days and nights to get to Bad Nauheim.

Marty and me at our wedding.

Our marriage certificate.

My dear sister, the only one survivor of my whole family. Only the two of us to share the heritage of our childhood, the cherished memory of all the past.

But Rella, when she heard of my marriage plans, immediately disapproved of them. "No nice Jewish girl gets involved with a soldier," she said. Soon Marty charmed her into a totally reversed attitude. She was with us and shared our happiness.

I was so fortunate to have my sister attend my wedding. I wanted very much to marry in the local synagogue—I think the only one that survived destruction in all of Germany. All of the rest had been burned and destroyed in the early years of war. Our wedding, however, was a bit of a national sensation and the press was keen to report on the story of the American GI and his Jewish survivor bride. Marty was the last person on earth to endure this sort of invasion of privacy, so we decided to avoid the synagogue, and married instead in the home of our friends Uta and Bernie.

Bad Nauheim was Uta's hometown (they now live in Buffalo, New York). She had married Bernie after the war. Both were camp survivors. Uta had repossessed her parents' old and beautiful home, after the war, and graciously offered it for our wedding reception. The home is on Ernst Ludwig Ring Strasse 10.

We encountered several problems with our marriage ceremonies. We married three times. A German civil ceremony took place first. We had to bribe with a few packs of cigarettes to open the courthouse because there was a local holiday on that December 11, the day

Cpl. Salinger Weds Polish Survivor in Offenbach, Germany

CPL. AND MRS. SALINGER'S MARRIAGE IN OFFENBACH

This photograph was taken at the marriage ceremony of Cpl. Martin Salinger of Detroit and Miss Mania Tannenbaum who was born in Radom, Poland, and survived Nazi persecutions and concentration camps.

The wedding was performed at Offenbach, Germany, on Dec. 12, and was attended by the bride's sister, Rella, and a number of their friends, young people and children who had survived the Nazi terror.

Cpl. Salinger met his bride at Bad-Nauheim, where she was secretary of the Jewish community, last September. He plans to bring her back with him to Detroit.

Stationed at Offenbach, Cpl. Salinger is prosecuting agent for the A.M.G. against Nazi perpetrators of atrocities.

Our wedding made the newspaper.

we planned to get married. We then had an American civil ceremony in Frankfort, but found that we were missing certain documents. We had our Jewish wedding ceremony planned for that same evening, but Marty was only able to obtain the documents the next day and the army chaplain who came from a distance to marry us waited in Bad Nauheim for the papers to clear. Our ceremony took place December 12.

My old friends from Pionki, the Kaplans, parents of little Tobie who was illegally hiding in Pionki, gave me away, managed the wedding reception, and offered their bedroom for our honeymoon night.

My life after that was filled with love, trust, much happiness, and Feven a few luxuries, including a private chauffeur. How impressed everyone was when he would drive me from where we lived in Offenbach to visit my sister and my friends in Bad Nauheim. How everyone catered now to the new Mrs. Salinger. Suddenly, I got exceptional treatment from the German hairdresser, the dressmaker, the maids, and the cooks.

The only problem that hampered our happy existence (besides the fact that we both wanted to get out of Germany and leave all the bad memories behind) was the fact that no permission was yet given by the army for a wife to live in the army quarters with her husband. Soldiers getting married overseas was a new phenomenon. We had to rent a room in a nearby German house. There we could spend most nights together. At times I sneaked into Marty's quarters but felt odd there, like a mistress.

Marty worked now in Offenbach as a prosecutor for the Military Government. He feared a reprisal from Germans connected to those whom he had helped put in jail. He encountered several scary incidents and slept with a gun under his pillow. One time as we passed through a German town someone fired at our car.

We could not leave Germany together, since he was still in the army. I was scheduled to leave by boat in May with all other war brides. Marty returned to the States in March as scheduled. After he left I anxiously awaited my departure and the beginning of my new life. We corresponded, of course. Recently I found a stack of letters that I had written to him, all in German, which Marty had saved all these years without ever telling me!

Eventually the time came. Goodbyes had to be said to so many dear friends, old and new. Leaving Germany behind meant leaving so many memories.

I remember our luxurious boat, filled with anxious war brides, crossing the ocean and the stormy seas. I remember the anticipation, the excitement! I remember waiters giving us English menus, which we could not understand, so we would just point to an item and wait with interest to see what we had ordered.

It was in the early hours of the morning when we approached our destination and had a first glimpse of the Statue of Liberty. A very special feeling overwhelmed me, as if the statue was lighting the way to a new life—life with a loving husband—in a new, free world.

We saw New York from a distance. It was the most exhilarating feeling I had ever experienced.

The boat landed. It took a while for the immigration officials to clear the red tape and every war bride whose name was called left to the waiting arms of her new husband. Finally my turn came and I saw Marty's outstretched arms and big "welcome home" smile. I felt like I truly was coming home after a lifetime of travel and an existence in another world.

We spent a few days in New York. It was all happening so fast! New York seemed like an impossible dream. I could hardly keep up with what was happening to me. It was so overwhelming and a bit scary. With much anticipation we boarded a train to Detroit. The whole family met us as the station in a big surprise family welcome. There were three brothers, a sister, sister-in-laws, and Aunt and Uncle Kraft.

I was scared. I knew that they would look at me with very critical eyes—this Jewish survivor from Poland who knew no Yiddish, no Hebrew, no English, had no known background, and was not even especially pretty. I thought that each one would be asking in their private thoughts, "What has Marty gotten himself into?"

Marty hugged me tightly, and introduced me with pride.

Aunt Fannie Kraft walked towards me with open arms and a warm welcome. My sister-in-law Adeline followed her and hugged me. The rest looked at me with curiosity and gave me a friendly greeting.

Uncle Harry Kraft had secured for us a small apartment—no small feat, for housing was very tight as all the homecoming GIs snapped it up.

My sister Rella married our cousin Leon in 1946, shortly after I married Marty. Leon had survived the war in Russia, where he lived until the war ended. They joined us in the US. I am so lucky to have them living near me still. My sister and I share a very close bond.

It is no exaggeration to say that, in the beginning, I was wholly overwhelmed. I didn't know how to cook, how to wash dishes, how to do laundry, or how to sweep the floor. I had never done it in Poland, not even in the camps. Marty, with patience and understanding, taught me the basics of housekeeping. I didn't even know how to handle American money. That was no problem for Marty. He gave me a large bill for groceries. I give him the change, then he would give me another large bill the next time. I never had to count out the change.

As I adjusted to American life, language, and cus-

War-bride class in Detroit, 1946-47.
I am in the first row, in the forefront.

toms, there were many incidents that stand out in my mind. One time, Marty showed me how to take the bus, but forgot to tell me to enter through the "entrance" door. I saw an open door and I went in through the exit— I almost got arrested. Another incident occurred during a dinner we had with his family. Someone openly criticized me for eating incorrectly. That was very embarrassing, and I was frustrated by the sheer numbers of things that I apparently had to learn in order to fit in.

But, I was not depressed. I was elated to be free, to be in such a wonderful country. I learned English and the "American" ways in a war-bride class. I attended an elementary school for an easy start with the language. The kids were surprised to see an adult that knew math but

This is the last photo taken of Marty, July 4, 1983.
He died three days later. (Marty, me, our daughter
Debbie, and her husband Jon.)

could not speak English. I was a quick learner, and five
months later I took a class at Wayne State University.

I was in love and I was loved. I realized what true
love is. In my previous life, in Radom, I had fallen into
the passionate infatuation that happens to young people
when they are first moved by another. Now, with Marty,
I experienced the deep feeling of belonging, of trust, of
someone to lean on, cry with, and laugh with. How good
it was to be in his arms.

I never realized until many, many years later how
fortunate I was to not have married a survivor. Two survivors who marry remember forever the tragedies of the
war and often they and their kids suffer depression for

years to come. With Marty, I could put the tragic past into the shadows.

I was married to Martin Salinger for thirty-seven years. Sadly, he died at the early age of sixty-five. He had wisdom and foresight, and I learned from him all my life. He was my lover, my best friend, and my teacher. I think of him often and sometimes I feel his presence.

I have little time to reflect on my past, but it's always there, in the shadows of my thoughts.

I have come to the end of my journal. Writing it was not an easy task, as I do not have writing skills or proper command of the English language.

I wrote it so many years ago and when I read it recently, I couldn't put it down. I seemed to have read about another me, in another lifetime. I added many pages. I tried to give you, dear reader, as vivid a picture as possible of my life in Poland: the sadness of war, and the happy ending. I suffered so much trauma. I witnessed so much death and destruction. I lost so many loved ones. I appreciate life; I appreciate living in the best country in the world, even with all her mistakes and failures. It's the country that gave me, and so many other survivors, the opportunity to start a new life, a good life.

Epilogue

I just finished my first meeting with Sarah, the editor who will critique my book. She is enthusiastic, and has gotten to know me now both in person and through my writing. I am hoping that you, the reader, will get to know me too. I poured my heart out in this book. I am told to write an epilogue. All of this was not an easy task.

I am not a writer; I haven't tried to put this in any literary form. I wrote it as if I were talking to my children. Those are all my thoughts, my words, all my remembrances.

I am eighty-two years old now. I have most of my life behind me. I am able to look openly and critically at myself.

I am sensitive, emotional, and I am a worrier.

I am sociable, thoughtful, and generous.

I am neat and an organizer.

I am too openly critical at times.

I am impatient. I cry easily.

I often have feelings of insecurity.

I love people and I am lucky to be liked, and often, loved.

I developed friendships that lasted a lifetime.

I found, to my amazement, a core of toughness—a fighting spirit and courage in me when time required it.

The war left many scars. I hope I am forgiven for all my shortcomings.

It's late now, and I am looking at the few photos I was able to find to include in the book. Photos from childhood, from war years, and shortly after. I look at them, reminiscing with sadness, with joy, with some regret, and many tears. It all seems like a lifetime ago.

My mind goes back to Radom, to my happy childhood years, to my parents who gave me such loving support.

My mind goes back to my close and loving childhood groups of friends, all uprooted, blown over the world. So very few left now: Bella Shore in New York, Helen and Leo Silvers in Florida, Marian Meryn in Vienna, and Henry Starkman in my neighborhood. We cherish our friendship. We speak often, but never about the past, always about today.

My mind goes back to the "sentimental journey" I took alone twenty-five years ago—a trip home to Radom. I stayed with our dear Christian friends, the Kubika family. They were as loving and welcoming as only a family could be. They went with me to visit the gymnasium (my high school). It was still an impressive building, and it stirred so many memories. The Kubikas also helped me find two treasured photos, which I enclosed in the book. They went with me to my old home at Zeromskiego 48. They watched over me, worrying about my safety (I was the only Jew in town) and my emotional state.

When I was at Zeromskiego 48, I stood there a long time. I looked at the kitchen window, closed my eyes, and could visualize my mother. With tears in my eyes I said goodbye to it all, and left.

My second husband, Mickey Hern, and me.

I've had a good, rich life. Leaving it would be sad, but I have no fear of death. My only fear is of helplessness and of becoming a burden to my loved ones.

I am alone now; widowed twice. After Marty passed away I was married to Mickey Hern for five years, a loving and charming man.

My accomplishments? My daughter Debbie speaks of her mother, ". . . learning to swim at fifty-five, learning to play bridge at sixty-five, and learning how to get on the internet at seventy-five."

I took over our corporation after Marty died, and succeeded in the men's business world. I have since retired from the business in 2005, but I miss working with figures and numbers and equations, and still look lovingly at an adding machine.

My regrets? Too numerous to mention. They give me many sleepless nights.

My accomplishment, the one I am most proud of—my family. I could write a whole chapter about my daughters, Susan, Joanie, and Debbie, and my dear son-in-

My three daughters: Susan, Debbie, and Joanie.

law, Jon. I am grateful for their love, understanding, and patience, for always being there when I needed them.

And I am so proud and grateful for my three grand-children. They are my dividend, my pride and joy. So hard to adequately describe my feelings! David, the oldest grandchild, graduated with honors from Brown and earned his masters in International Relations from Johns Hopkins University. His interest is in Eastern Europe, where his grandma is from. I hope that, even if it is in a small way, David will be able to contribute to a better world. David calls and writes, and some of his notes I keep in a special place. He wrote recently, "You've become the matriarch of a large family and your example has helped shape us into a better people. Thanks for always being there."

My pride and joy, my three grandchildren:
Marni, David, and Eli.

The three greatest guys: David, Eli,
and my son-in-law, Jon.

Marni, my sweet and only granddaughter. She's an exceptional student, champion swimmer, a busy member of Habonim (the same youth group her grandpa Marty was so active in—how proud he would have been). My Marni—my shining, bright teenager. Always busy and always loving her "mini" grandma.

Eli, the youngest. He is such a delightful, loving, kissing little boy. Brilliant Hillel student, busy with soccer, piano, and chess. At age six he worried about me being lonely and assured me, "I will always love you no matter what."

I lead a busy life filled with many activities. I play bridge, I swim, I read. I am a member of IRP (Institute of Retired Professionals). It is uplifting to be in the company of such bright people.

I spend winters in Scotsdale, Arizona. I am lucky not to have to endure the harsh winters here in Michigan. I have many friends and manage, despite the pains and aches, to lead a busy social life there too.

I am a Holocaust Survivor Speaker at our new, beautiful Holocaust Memorial Center here in Farmington Hills, Michigan. I meet with groups of children and adults of many faiths. I tell stories about sorrow, about suffering, about hope, and about courage. It is not easy to recall the tragic times over and over again and not let it fade away. I try to talk about another Mania, in another lifetime. I see tears in people's eyes, I see smiles when I tell a hopeful story, I get hugs and kisses and praises and blessings. I get many thank-you notes, some that touch my heart. "Thank you for your willingness not to forget so that we may remember," wrote Mrs. Darla Lyons from Chapel Hill Christian School in Ohio.

I hope that people will understand and remember this tragic chapter of our history, and never allow it to happen again, to any group of people.

I began writing my memoirs twenty-five years ago. Reading, adding, correcting, discussing, and editing it to create a publishable book puts an enormous strain on me. I get tense. I cry. I have sleepless nights when I am awake thinking and remembering what was then and what could have been now. I keep thinking in a broader sense what was lost to society. So many people lost to the world. We live in such turbulent and violent times. Perhaps some of them could have helped make a safer and more beautiful place for us all to live in.